Basic Preparedness

Written By
The Survival Center, Inc.

Published By The Survival Center, Inc.
P.O. Box 234
McKenna, WA 98558

New Revised Edition
Copyright © 1995 The Survival Center, Inc.

Cover Design © 1995 The Survival Center, Inc.

ISBN 0-9642342-0-3

Disclaimer

This book is designed to provide accurate and authoritative information in regard to the subject matter covered. It is sold with the understanding that the publisher and author are not engaged in rendering legal, medical, electrical, plumbing, general contracting or other professional services. If this advice or other expert assistance are required, the services of a competent professional should be sought.

It is not the purpose of this manual to reprint all the information that is otherwise available on the various subjects addressed, and for more detailed information see the reference section.

Every effort has been made to make this book as complete and as accurate as possible. However, there may be mistakes both typographical and in content. Therefore, this text should be used only as a general guide and not as the ultimate source of writing.

The purpose of this book is to educate. The author nor publisher shall have neither liability nor responsibility to any person or entity with respect to any loss or damage caused or alleged to be caused directly or indirectly by the information contained in this book.

TABLE OF CONTENTS

WHY BOTHER WITH SURVIVAL PREPARATION?

There are a number of different scenarios that would necessitate the need for food and water storage, medical supplies and alternative housing. These include:

1. **Earthquake**
2. **Flooding**
3. **Severe Winter Storm**
4. **Tornado**
5. **Hurricane**
6. **Volcanic Eruption**
7. **Economic Collapse**
8. **Nuclear Accident or Attack**
9. **Biological Warfare**
10. **Civil Unrest - Riots, Trucker's Strike or Earth Changes, Etc.**
11. **Toxic Food Supply**
12. **Food Shortages (world reserves currently less than 30 days)**

If any one of these disasters struck today, you could be without electricity for possibly weeks. If you live in the city this means you could be without water, light and heat for an indefinite period of time.

Never assume it can't happen here. Only two generations ago most families put up food for a long winter and lived close to the land with readily available water from a hand pumped well. These families survived the Great Depression and were untouched by natural weather problems.

We have become so used to modern conveniences and dependency on government agencies for water, power and our livelihood that we have completely forgotten how to survive even the simplest of power outages. It would not take a terribly violent earthquake to disrupt the power within a large metropolitan area for an extended period of time, as has already been demonstrated.

Preparation for any kind of emergency is just good common sense and another form of insurance. Most people have medical, dental, fire, theft, homeowners and automobile insurance, yet they lack the basic insurance of essential survival, food and water. There is no government agency that is going to provide you with the essential food and water necessary in the event of a natural or economic disaster. A truly comprehensive insurance plan would include storing food, water, outdoor survival gear and medical supplies.

Because basic survival has never been taught in the public school system most people are ignorant and confused about what the necessary survival needs are.

This book was created to give a comprehensive guide to all of the basic necessary survival needs and skills that will secure you and your family in the event of any kind of disaster, short or long term. This one reference guide will answer most of your questions. If you want more information on any subject, we have additional volumes that explore in depth all of your basic survival needs.

EMERGENCY EXERCISES

One good way to test you and your family on how prepared you are for any kind of emergency is to try one of the following exercises. You never really know how you will react to a situation unless you are forced to experience it for yourself.

There are several types of emergency situations, those that are temporary and last only a few days, those that last a few weeks and those that are long term. Let's have a dress rehearsal. The following are some potential ways to test your readiness:

1.   Weekend Scenario

A storm has just blown through your area and it is Friday night. All the family is at home. The storm has created a total power outage. On your battery operated radio you are told by the news bureau that you will be without power for the entire weekend. Trees are down and you cannot use your vehicle so you are confined to your home. Also consider the fact that this could happen during winter, when you are the most vulnerable to the elements. To duplicate the above scenario you and your family could try the following exercise.

Begin Friday evening by turning off your electrical power, water main and gas line, if you have one. In other words disable your utilities. We are now duplicating an emergency when all the power will be no longer available. The test is to see how well you can function without power for cooking, heating, lighting, washing, the basics for a comfortable lifestyle. Since you will be unable to travel you will also be dependent only upon the food you have available. What would you do?

2.   Week Long Scenario

An earthquake, hurricane or tornado has struck your area. All major utilities are totally disabled and will not be functional for at least one week. This includes the telephone. The roads are damaged and you are unable to travel to acquire any new supplies. There is minor damage to your property. How would you handle being confined to your home without power, water, or access to more food for a week or more? Some family members were not at home during this disaster. What is your back-up communications plan? Does each family member know what to do wherever they are? See Earthquake - Emergency Checklist on page 180 for more information.

3.   Long Term Disaster

A nuclear war, biological warfare, earth changes or a total economic collapse, disables the entire social structure economically and politically for a long time. You have no power, water, telephone, access to food, new supplies or travel. You and your family are confined to your property and there is no assistance from the government or other agencies to aid in your survival efforts. You do not have a fallout shelter or other device to protect yourself from biological or nuclear radiation. Your home has sustained some damage and you have medical emergencies to take care of with some family members. What do you do? For suggestions on how to withstand this kind of disaster see Earthquake - Emergency Checklist on page 180.

If you are unsure as to how prepared you are for any type of emergency, you should assess your current supply of food, water and sanitation necessities and see how long you could survive if it were suddenly impossible to restock your cupboards. Most people would be very surprised at the short length of time they could survive if they were dependent only upon their stock on hand.

It is possible to prepare for this or other kinds of emergency disasters. If you are properly prepared materially and psychologically you will be not only able to survive the above scenarios adequately, you will be able to be relatively comfortable during an emergency situation. You will also potentially be of benefit to others who are less prepared.

INTRODUCTION

This book has been compiled to meet a growing need for self-sufficiency, an idea that is spreading rapidly among people who are waking up to the reality of today's chaotic economic, geologic and political climate. There are many reference books on the market that can help you create sovereignty and secure you and your family for the times that are here now and ahead. But, therein lies the problem. There are many many books and most of us are too busy attempting to prepare for our financial future. Reading a myriad of different books is out of the question for most, but building a library for future use is essential. This book will help you to eliminate the costly research and time necessary to reading all of these books now. The Survival Center has been in business for 20 plus years. In this time we have researched and gained extensive knowledge and combined experience in all areas of survival. This book will assist you getting a start on the basics.

It is finally time to have all the pertinent basic information in one place, presented in a cohesive format. To be able to go to one source of information in your efforts to prepare yourself for an uncertain future is greatly needed. We decided to fulfill that need. We have purposely kept this book to the essential survival needs. It would take volumes to go into elaborate detail. We want to keep it simple.

We have over a century of combined experience among those who are contributing to this reference material. We not only have the expertise to fulfill your survival needs, we can supply you with, or point you to the necessary supplies and materials to complete all of your self-sufficiency projects.

The four basics in preparing for any potential future are:

1. **Food**
2. **Water**
3. **Medical**
4. **Shelter**

1.   **Food:** A minimum of one year and preferably two or more year's supply of food, stored properly and on hand for any emergency will sustain you and your family, regardless of what happens with the world's political, economic or weather situation. See chart on page 13.

2.   **Water:** A clean source of water is absolutely essential to survival. If at all possible your should have your own well that has the option for hand pumping operation. If this is not possible, you should store at least several hundred gallons of purified water for an emergency predicament, along with portable water filters.

3.   **Medical:** There are basic medical and sanitation supplies that should be kept readily available to handle any health or medical emergency. You should be familiar with an emergency medical kit and how to use it. Keep at least one comprehensive kit at home. There are also simple things that one can do on a daily basis to help keep the body detoxified and maintained in optimum health. If you are dependent on any medications or prescriptions you need to have an extra supply on hand. Lack of running water, electricity, and functional toilet facilities make sanitation a primary consideration in any emergency (short or long term). Be sure to stock up on sanitation supplies (bacterial soap, extra water, moist towelettes, alcohol swab/pads, paper towels, rubber gloves etc.) and remember to keep your hands clean when performing first aid and preparing food.

To maintain one's health with proper sanitary practices during an emergency, soap and home cleaning products are a must. Have an ample supply stored. There are many household products you use every day that can be made from simple ingredients. The advantage to making these simple cleaning products and household agents is that they do not have the toxic ingredients that the industry uses that cause allergic reactions or compromises health. Plus, they are more economical and environmentally friendly because of their natural ingredients. They don't require new packaging. Basic soap, toothpaste, household cleaning agents, hair care and cosmetics are simply made from natural ingredients and herbs. Learn how to create your own in Chapter 9.

4.   **Shelter:** If at all possible the first prerequisite to having a stable survival situation is to have property or some place to go outside of the city. It will be very difficult to survive in the cities during any kind of natural, political or economic disaster. You can imagine the picture of panic and desperation that will ensue for large numbers of people suddenly in a position of having no electricity, therefore, no water and very little food on hand. The evening news has shown many cities cut off by man-made or natural disasters. Learn from these real life examples and prepare now, while costs are still stable.

Having an alternative shelter in a rural area is the answer to removing yourself and your family from the chaos that will prevail in the cities. If you are able to make a permanent move to a rural area you can begin to live self-sufficiently. It would also be wise to build an underground shelter that could sustain you and your family during any kind of natural or political disaster. There are many ways to approach this, from a simple root cellar type of dwelling, to the more elaborate models used by the military. This book will present many alternative forms of shelter.

There are some simple and basic tools that every home needs to maintain fundamental repairs. It is important to have non-electric tools wherever possible and non-electric appliances, like a hand operated grain mill, propane stove, etc. Assume that the power will be turned off for extended periods of time. Unless you have created your own free energy or solar device you must rely on human power to do household and mechanical repairs. Know what to have on hand and how to use it for your particular situation.

Various forms of alternative energy are available. If you would like to run certain household appliances or a well pump from electricity, you can purchase and maintain a generator. Solar power is also a consideration and can run many appliances and fixtures if properly installed. A combination of solar and a generator is advisable in most cases, in the event that one system fails.

In a sudden economic, political or natural disaster there will be great chaos. People who have not prepared will be desperate for food, water and some form of shelter, and those injured will need medical care. This could create a serious problem for those who have prepared and need to protect themselves from dangerous intruders. There are many weapons on the market. You need to know which weapon would be best for your particular situation. In a rural setting you need to know what weapons, including cross bows, etc., are best for hunting game or fishing.

Many methods of camouflaging can be used to hide either you or your homestead. If you are truly prudent you can create an environment of invisibility for yourself and family, so that it will be unnecessary to fend off intruders, either in the form of people in panic or a government out of control.

What does self-sufficiency mean? Webster's dictionary defines it as the "ability to maintain oneself without outside aid: capable of providing for one's own needs." In practical terms this can refer to the ability to run your home, i.e. cooking, pumping water, lights, etc., without electricity. (Remember rural electrification only started approximately 50 years ago). It can also refer to your ability to produce your own food supply, be it fruit, vegetables, dairy or meat.

What self-sufficiency also means is becoming disconnected from public utilities, the mass food supply, the current medical system and providing these things on your own. Basically it means going back to the land and living as our grandparents did. Returning to life without dependency on electricity or oil, living with the natural environment and reaping the benefits that nature so abundantly supplies. It can be done! And, there is a wonderful sense of personal empowerment that comes as a result. Now you have the joy of realized independence. This makes more options available to you.

The ability to be totally self-sufficient creates a condition of sovereignty. Sovereignty equates freedom or dominion over one's life and lifestyle. With adequate preparation every individual can become free of any kind of interference in their affairs. Coming together in small groups or communities of like-minded people can be very beneficial for all. But, if that's not an option for you, don't let that keep you from doing something on your own. We will present various options to setting up a completely independent lifestyle, you can choose the methods that apply to your personal situation. Every great journey begins with a single step. The most important thing to do is take that step and keep going. Nothing is more powerful than an idea whose time has come. <u>Now</u> is that time - <u>Let's do more than "Just Survive"</u>.

Food Storage

Food Storage Basics

There is a notion about food storage that by simply storing wheat, milk, salt, sugar or honey, that this will be sufficient for survival in hard times. <u>This idea is false</u>. We have had 20 plus years of research and experience in this area, and we firmly believe that you need a variety of foods and lots of it. Wheat, milk, salt, sugar or honey will not provide you with the necessary protein, vitamins, minerals, amino acids and other essential nutrients. Depending upon the reason for survival; earthquake, nuclear accident, biological warfare, economic collapse, etc., there will be a great deal of work to do to rebuild and sustain even a simple lifestyle. Extraordinary amounts of energy and mental clarity are required in a stressful situation. You need all of the nourishment you can obtain. You definitely cannot sustain the body under such conditions, with a poor diet.

We have provided a **Food Storage Basics For One Year** chart on the following page. This chart gives an accurate picture of the quantities of food that will be necessary for a family to properly nourish themselves during and beyond a crisis situation. You should also consider storing an adequate amount of herbs and homeopathic supplies, as these are excellent for many medicinal purposes. Storing vitamins and minerals is a great idea also. Remember that your stored items are only as valuable as your ability to use them effectively. Many of our staff have used and consumed over the last 20+ years many of the items recommended for storage. We have years of first hand practical experience on what works and what doesn't to help you along the way.

FOOD STORAGE BASICS FOR ONE YEAR

BASIC MINIMUM FOOD, WATER STORAGE AND RELATED ITEMS ©1993 Survival Center, Inc.	Quantity in Pounds Required Per Family Member (Rounded to nearest lb.)						TOTAL BASICS NEEDED FOR YOUR FAMILY Figure Your Needs Here
	1-6 Child	7-12 Child	13-15 Teen	16+ Teen	M Adult	F Adult	
Wheat, hard red winter	115	225	240	295	350	250	
Honey, molasses, maple syrup	20	30	35	45	60	50	
Nonfat dried milk	85	100	100	110	75	60	
Salt - If curing meat store extra	3	5	7	5	10-20	10-20	
Grains: corn, barley, oats, rice, millet, rye etc.	55	95	125	145	155	120	
Dried beans, lentils, soybeans, peas, pinto, kidney, etc.	15	20	35	45	55	45	
Selection of dried vegetables, carrots, corn, peas, green beans, etc.	25	40	40	50	45	35	
Potato granules, slices, dices	25	55	65	95	60	60	
Selection of Air and Freeze Dried, Main Course Entrees. Convert to #10 can equivalents	6-10 cans or 20 lbs.	6-11 cans or 30 lbs.	7-12 cans or 45 lbs.	7-12 cans or 55 lbs.	6-11 cans or 30 lbs.	6-10 cans or 25 lbs.	
Dried fruit + Orange or Apple Drink Powder	65	90	90	120	85	75	
Your choice of canned meats+ TVP, MRE's, etc.	5	20	20	55	45	35	
Gelatin, margarine pwd., butter pwd., tapioca, powdered eggs	10	15	20	30	30	20	
Cheese Powder, Peanut Butter + Peanut Butter Pwd.	15	15	20	25	25	20	
Olive Oil, Salad oils, Vegetable shortening	18	25	35	45	30	25	
Vitamins, Minerals, Herbs	Check with your health practitioner for information on these storage items. Most manufacturers we talked to said their product would have full potency for 2 - 3 yrs.						
Water (1 gal. per person per day, min. - cook & drink only)	365 Gal.	365 Gal.	365 Gal.	365 Gal.	365 Gal.	365 Gal.	
Sprouting Seeds -Soap -Water Purifier - Bleach - H₂0₂	Herbs, Spirulina, Seaweed, (Kombu, Dulce, Nori) Cooking Spices, Miso						

Nutritive and Storage Life Chart

TYPE OF FOOD	NUTRITIVE VALUE	ROTATION NECES-SARY	NUTRITIVE SHELF LIFE	STORAGE SHELF LIFE	TASTE AND EYE APPEAL	PREPARA-TION TIME	PRESER-VATIVES	SPACE	COST	WEIGHT	ADDITIONAL FOOD NEEDED FOR PREPARA-TION OF MAIN COURSE ITEMS	SOURCE OF REAL MEATS
FREEZE DRIED	GREAT as good as fresh frozen	NO	at least 10 years plus ★	very possibly indefinitely 15+ yrs.	GREAT like fresh or frozen	0 - 10 min.	NO freeze drying process preserves ★★★	about same space as original food	Initial cost appears greater than air dried or grains but all factors must be considered	VERY LIGHT over 90% original weight removed	NO just add water	YES
AIR DRIED Dehydrated	GOOD some loss due to heat processing	YES	4 - 7 years ★	4 - 15 years	some loss of original color and fresh taste	20 min. several hours	USUALLY read labels	slightly less space than original food but expands when cooked	LESS expensive than freeze dried	slightly heavier than freeze dried	YES	NO
GRAINS, BEANS, SEEDS, LEGUMES	VERY HIGH	NO	INDEFINITE ★ 15-20+	INDEFINITE ★★ 15-20+	GREAT become familiar with them	20 min. several hours	NO	same as original but expands when cooked	BEST BUY FOR YOUR MONEY	Heavier than air dried or freeze dried	YES	NO
CANNED GOODS COMMER-CIAL AND HOME	FAIR TO POOR	YES	6 months to one year	3 years	FAIR	NONE usually except for warming	Sometimes, check label	POOR wasted space due to excess moisture	POOR when all things considered	Very Heavy	YES	YES. but not for storage

★ Storage Life affected by temperature - 70ºF or below preferred. ©1993 Survival Center, Inc.

★★Brown Rice is not recommended for long term storage. Rotate every two years.

★★★With the exception of carrots, apples and mushrooms which have additives to protect color

Food Processing and Preservation Comparison Sheet

The following information provides some comparisons between various methods of food processing and preservation. Here are the common ways to preserve and/or store food, not in any particular order.

A) Fresh (refrigeration)
B) Home canning and bottling
C) Home dehydration by air or oven drying
D) Commercial dehydration and packaging, using vacuum or air drying

E) Freezing (home and/or commercial)
F) Commercial canning and bottling
G) Commercial freeze drying and packaging

Below are the advantages and disadvantages of each method or preserving food for storage?

ADVANTAGES	DISADVANTAGES
FRESH	
Best Tasting	Will not store in fresh state for long period, thus not available year round.
Most nutritious	Loses nutritional value if not used very soon after harvest
	Can takes time to prepare (peeling, slicing, dicing, shredding, etc.)
HOME CANNING & BOTTLING	
Relatively easy to do.	Storage life is usually only certain for 1-2 years maximum.
Can be economical after equipment and jars are purchased.	Bottles can break, lids do not always seal.
	Time consuming and nutrient loss due to heat.
	Some foods lose a considerable amount of the original taste, appearance and nutritional value.
	Potential health hazard, if improperly done.
FREEZING	
Retains high percentage of nutritional value.	Storage life varies from 6 months to 2 years only.
Easy to do at home if freezer is available.	Power shortage can ruin entire freezer full of food.
Retains fresh color, shape, etc.	Initial investment in a freezer can be expensive.
Food tastes almost like fresh.	Must be rotated and used up.
COMMERCIAL CANNING (Wet Pack)	
Convenient, familiar easy to buy at grocery stores.	Limited storage life - 6 months to 3 years maximum.
Almost unlimited variety available.	Must be rotated and used up.
Stores easily in kitchen pantry.	Foods contain water - you are storing extra weight.
Easy to prepare.	Low nutritional value/processed at high heat.
HOME DEHYDRATING AND DRYING	
Convenient	Skill is needed in order to dry and still retain nutritional value.
Easy to do at home.	Packaging and storage critical.

Chart continued

Continued from previous page

ADVANTAGES	DISADVANTAGES
No refrigeration needed to store.	Must avoid extended high heat and cooking to maintain nutrients.
Home dried food will last for years if done properly.	1-3 years average shelf life - commercially packed lasts longer.
Preservatives not needed.	Some foods will discolor slightly.
Nutrient value, next best compared to fresh and freeze dried.	Sometimes less appealing to look at.
This makes home drying high on the list. It is easy with some practice, and you know the quality of what you started with.	Can require reconstituting and cooking time.
COMMERCIAL DRYING, DEHYDRATION AND PACKAGING	
Food shrivels or shrinks to a smaller size - more food can be stored in a smaller place.	Packaging methods vary - some seal cans with air in can - many try to nitrogen pack, but do not have proper know-how and testing equipment, therefore, leaving high levels of oxygen in cans. Oxygen absorbing packets not the answer.
This food is usually offered in #10 can size	Skill is needed in order to dry and still retain nutritional value. Nutrient loss due to heat used in processing.
Stores for many years - 5 - 12 years.	Much soaking and cooking is needed which lessens nutritional values. Some sulphides used to retain color.
Dry weight may be as little as 10% of the fresh weight.	Tends to lose more nutritional content than does fresh, frozen or freeze dried foods, if not properly packaged.
FREEZE DRYING AND PACKAGING	
No refrigeration needed.	Because the food does not shrivel, but retains its normal size and cell structure, you need more space than is required for dehydrated.
Storage life of many years if properly sealed. 10 - 15 years.	Basic cost per dry ounce is usually higher than other processes - however, less water, less fuel, and much less time is needed to prepare the food. Thus, the total cost for prepared - ready to eat food is relatively the same as dehydrated in most cases.
Dry weight may be as little 10% of the fresh weight.	
Most of these foods can be prepared with hot or cold water in less than 5 min. without the need for cooking - the ultimate in convenience.	
Preservatives are not needed or used in most cases.	Some sulphides are used to retain color - check label.
When compared in years of storage - replacement of other foods such as frozen or canned, cost more than a readily available supply of Freeze Dried Foods.	
Freeze drying retains more of the natural fresh flavor and nutrition than any other dehydration process.	Some MSG used as flavor enhancer - check label.
A great way to store meat for years 5 -10 plus.	More expensive.

16

Different Methods For Storing Food

Freeze Drying - Freeze drying is vacuum sublimation. Foods are flash frozen at -50°F, then placed in a vacuum chamber where radiant heat is applied to turn the frozen water content directly into a vapor, which is literally vacuumed away. The vacuum is broken with nitrogen, which replaces any oxygen remaining and the contents are then sealed in their special heavy duty containers. Less than 2% oxygen and 2% moisture remain. These are standard requirements for the military as they provide one of the longest shelf live's available for stored food. The average life for freeze-dried food is 7 - 15 years.

Air Dried - Home air dried food is the simplest and most natural way to preserve your food. It is the least costly method of home food preservation. Air drying saves time, energy, storage space and the cost of equipment is low.

To air dry food you simply cut up the food and dry it. Thin slices, dices or strips will dry more quickly. Some items, like your favorite fruit, you may want to be thicker and more moist and therefore more succulent and easy to chew. When dry, store your food in air tight containers in a cool, dark place. Plastic bags, used yogurt containers, peanut butter jars and just about anything air tight will keep your dried food for many months. Always store in a cool dark place for maximum shelf life. It is wise to periodically check your air dried food in the beginning to see if any moisture has penetrated the sealed containers. Moisture will spoil the food and ruin it for long term storage.

Air drying need not be complicated. The simpler the better. Experience has taught that one does not need all the blanching, steaming and sulphides as suggested in the past. If you feel the need to use something to preserve color of apples, etc., a weak solution of ascorbic acid (vitamin C crystals) or lemon juice can be used as a predrying dip. Have fun, save time, save energy and end up with a healthy dried food made at home by doing it yourself. <u>Remember K.I.S.- Keep It Simple!</u>

Dehydration by air involves processing foods at low heating temperatures. Much of the water is removed, the food's cell structure is somewhat altered, the food shrivels and is finally dehydrated. Some food must then be soaked and/or cooked for up to 15 - 20 min. before it is rehydrated and ready to eat, unless you are eating it dry as a snack. Modern methods and home drying appliances have greatly improved in the last several years. It is much easier and more of the nutrients are retained.

Both freeze dried and air dried foods retain more of their original nutrition than do foods stored using other methods. Certain foods like meat cannot be satisfactorily dehydrated and retain a lengthy shelf life. Freeze drying is the only way to keep meat for long term storage, 5 - 10 yrs +.

Test Results - In the summer of 1993 our staff initiated laboratory testing of five of the leading food storage manufacturer's products. Products tested were air dried and freeze dried foods packaged in #10 cans. The test was for oxygen content, which is critical to the long shelf life of these foods. Oxygen and moisture contents of less than 2% offer the longest possible shelf life, as indicted by commercial and military testing. Oxygen contents of less than 2% are required by the military on all air dried and freeze dried foods purchased for military food storage. This is known as military specifications or MIL-SPEC. Of the five leading brands tested, only two met these requirements of less than 2% oxygen.

Some manufacturers feel the oxygen absorbing packets will solve this problem. However, our tests have proven that this is not true. It is in the specific vacuum and nitrogen flushing process that the oxygen is removed. The oxygen absorbing packets are insufficient to remove all oxygen.

Nitrogen Packing

Nitrogen packing has been used in the food storage industry since its inception. Nitrogen is an inert gas and won't react with foods. Nitrogen replaces the residual oxygen in the food container. It is oxygen that creates spoilage. Food to be stored in #2 1/2 and #10 cans should be vacuum packed first, and then nitrogen is backflushed in the container to prevent oxygen retention. Some manufacturers do not vacuum first.

Food packed in poly buckets is normally nitrogen packed, but not vacuum packed. Some manufacturers do not use nitrogen either. Please check your source before any purchases. Poly buckets are commonly used in the storage of grains, beans, seeds and legumes for economy and convenience. There are many other uses of poly buckets once they have been emptied of food. See page 120 for more uses.

Poly Buckets

Poly Buckets (made of food grade High Density Polyethylene) are the 6 gallon food grade buckets that most nitrogen packed grains and legumes come packed in. This is the most efficient and economical way to store food long term. These buckets have a strong, permanent sealing lid that won't permit oxygen or moisture to enter the bucket once it is sealed. They can be stacked one upon the other to maximize storage space. If stacking more than 3 high, a board should be placed between every second layer. Thus the second, fourth and sixth buckets should have a board between them.

METHODS OF HOME FOOD DRYING

SUN DRYING - This is one of the oldest methods, but is practical only in areas of hot, continuous sun and dry air. You will probably need to build your own unit to sun dry, as commercial units are normally difficult to find. Be sure to cover top and bottom of food to dry with a suitable screen or cheese cloth to deter insects.

SMOKE HOUSE - This is a more controlled version of the open fire drying method used by the Indians. Normally used for meats; hams, bacon, etc. to help preserve for winter usage. Shelf life is limited to 6 - 12 months. This is another old-time method similar to sun drying that still has value and should be considered.

ELECTRIC DEHYDRATOR - The easiest and quickest way to dehydrate any time, any where - provided you have electricity. The basics are a container (box with trays) to hold the food, a controlled heat source and a fan to move the air. You can build your own or buy a commercially built one. The round commercial driers have worked best throughout our years of testing.

OVEN DRYING - This is an inexpensive way to get started with heat drying food. Be sure to keep the temperature low - 90 - 125° - and leave the oven door slightly ajar to circulate air. Remember the idea is to dry the food, not cook it.

MICROWAVE OVEN - This does not work well due to hot spots in the oven and the almost instant "cooking" of the food. The food may burn before drying, although some herbs have been successfully dried in a microwave.

PAPER BAG OR MESH BAG - The hot summer attic was a popular way to dry some fruits, vegetables or herbs. The food was hung from the rafters and dried well in either a paper bag or a mesh bag.

FRUIT LEATHERS - This is simply any fruit ground up (blender works best) into as dry a liquid as possible and poured out onto a special drying tray that will hold liquid. Cookie sheets work well if they have a Teflon coating to prevent sticking. Be sure to see that the liquid is no more than one eighth (1/8) thick in the tray so that it dries evenly. Put the tray in dehydrator or oven at low heat with the door ajar. When done, leather resembles a thin sheet of leather. Roll leather off the tray and store in between layers of clear wrap or wax paper, in a cool, dark and dry place. Kids love fruit leathers as a healthy snack and they are free of sugar or preservatives, unless you add them.

POWDERED DEHYDRATED VEGETABLES & FRUITS - Vegetables and fruits can be powdered after they are dehydrated by pulverizing in a blender. They can be used for purees, making soup or baby food, and are terrific space savers.

JERKY - This is dried and seasoned meat that is eaten in its dry state, not reconstituted or cooked. Jerky is easy to make in a dehydrator or oven. Slice the meat thin and place on racks, drying at a low temperature 110 - 130° until the meat is thoroughly dry and leathery. Make sure all the fat is trimmed off so that the meat will not turn rancid. Other parts of the animal can be turned into jerky, such as the liver and heart.

Any heat source could work; like a wood stove, furnace duct vents, or refrigerator heat vent, etc. Remember, too high a temperature destroys nutrient value and adequate air circulation allows the produce to dry more evenly. Even corn can be hung upside down by the peeled husk, and dried in the attic.

Home food dehydration can be fun, economical and a source of high quality food. Taking advantage of sales, bumper crops and surpluses will save you lots of dollars. Properly dried and stored, your home dehydrated food could last for years. One batch of our test apples (dried 4.5 years ago) which have been slowly consumed, still remain very dry and taste great. Check the reference section at the end of this book for a list of publications that go into greater detail on the food drying process.

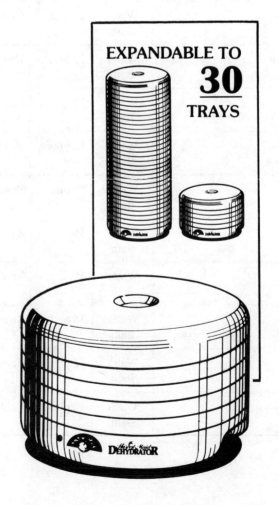

EXPANDABLE TO
30
TRAYS

APPROX. SHELF LIFE OF WET PACK CANNED FRUITS & VEGETABLES STORED AT @ 70° OR LESS

Produce	Method of Canning	Shelf Life in mos	Produce	Method of Canning	Shelf Life in mos
Apples & applesauce	Water Bath	36	Asparagus	Pressure	36 plus
Apricots	Water Bath	36	Beans, lima	Pressure	96 plus
Blackberries	Water Bath	12 plus	Beans, stringless	Pressure	36 plus
Blueberries	Water Bath	12 plus	Beet	Pressure	48 plus
Cherries, maraschino	Water Bath	12 plus	Brussel sprouts	Pressure	48 plus
Cherries, sweet	Water Bath	12 plus	Carrots	Pressure	96 plus
Cherries, black	Water Bath	12 plus	Corn	Pressure	96 plus
Cranberry sauce	Water Bath	12 plus	Hominy	Pressure	96 plus
Fruit salad	Water Bath	36	Peas	Pressure	96 plus
Grapes	Water Bath	12 plus	Pickles	Pressure	12 plus
Grapefruit	Water Bath	36 plus	Pumpkin and squash	Pressure	48 plus
Peaches	Water Bath	36	Sauerkraut	Pressure	12 plus
Pears	Water Bath	36	Spinach	Pressure	36 plus
Pineapple	Water Bath	36	Sweet potatoes	Pressure	48 plus
Plums	Water Bath	12 plus	Tomatoes	Water Bath	48 plus
Rhubarb	Water Bath	12 plus	Cabbage	Pressure	48 plus

Microorganisms

There are three types of microorganism: molds, yeast and bacteria that will contribute to the spoilage of foods. These microorganisms are found in water, air and in the ground. For a better understanding of these three we will explain each below:

- **MOLDS** - Molds are a downy, furry growth. When there is dampness or decay they are found on the surface of organic matter. They are caused by fungi. Boiling heat will destroy molds. They become inactive in temperatures under 32°F.

- **YEASTS** - Fermentation causes this fungi to create food spoilage. They are inactive at 0°F and below, but a temperature of 240° will ensure that they are no longer active.

- **BACTERIA** - Bacteria can be either good or bad. The bacteria we are concerned about are those that spoil food and meat. Decaying bacteria is evidenced by soft, slimy and flat sour food. Bacteria are the most stubborn of microorganisms to destroy. If they are not destroyed in the canning process they will continue to grow. Growth of bacteria ceases below 32°F and most bacteria cells are killed at 190°F. The spores may live beyond these temperatures and must be destroyed at a temperature of 240°F. The most deadly bacteria is the one causing botulism.

- **BOTULISM** - is caused by the bacteria spores of *clostridium botulinum*. They have the ability to grow in moist foods when oxygen is not present. Therefore, they can grow in your vacuum sealed jars if they are not properly canned. Their spores require a temperature of 240°F to be destroyed. All canned food should be boiled for twenty minutes in an open saucepan. If there is any botulism present it will be killed. If you detect an odor from your food upon opening do not eat the food. However, botulism does not necessarily cause a bad odor. Be sure the vacuum jar exhibits a popping sound when opening and breaking the seal.

Dairy Products

Powdered Milk

There are a number of dairy products that are useful to place in your food storage program. Powdered milk is one of them. Milk is a necessary ingredient in many recipes and has essential proteins not found in other foods. Non-Fat, non-instant, dry milk is recommended as it has a low moisture content and a long storage life.

The most useful is regular nonfat dry milk. It does require some stirring to blend into recipes very easily. Instant dry milk, on the other hand, reconstitutes easily but is highly processed, and therefore, much lower in nutrition. Powdered milk also allows you to make cottage cheese, yogurt, cream cheese and a variety of hard cheeses. Regular non-fat milk has an approximate nutrient shelf life of five years, but will store almost indefinitely.

Eggs

Eggs are an excellent source of protein in the diet. In fact, fertilized eggs have all of the essential 22 amino acids present, while unfertilized eggs are missing two amino acids. Many recipes call for eggs, and in fact, some recipes are impossible to make without eggs. Although one can live without eggs they are a staple for most people, and fortunately, there are ways to have them when the chickens aren't laying. Eggs can supply many of the essential amino acids, and B vitamins that could otherwise be lacking in the diet.

Most people are not familiar with various methods of storing eggs. Eggs stored in their cartons will keep at refrigerator temperatures for 4 to 5 weeks, but their freshness fades as time passes. Eggs lose carbon dioxide and water, which causes them to spread out more when they are broken open. The best way to test the freshness of an egg is to place it in a bowl of water. If the egg sinks to the bottom it is fresh. If it rises to the top and floats it is spoiled and should be discarded.

One of the original methods of storing eggs was to place them inside a large barrel filled with dry salt, which is then stored in a cellar or springhouse to keep cool. The essential element to keeping eggs is to clog up the pours of the shell so that oxygen does not enter the shell. Various methods of rubbing grease, zinc, or boric ointment have proven successful.

The Waterglass method is the use of sodium silicate to seal the shells. Fill a crock with eggs that are at least 12 hours old. Mix the sodium silicate (which you can buy at any pharmacy) at a percentage of 1 part sodium silicate to 11 parts water. This will take on a gelled consistency. Immerse the eggs in this mixture inside a large crock and store in a cool place. The only drawback to the waterglass method is that these eggs will not be good for any recipe that uses eggs for rising. The whites will be very watery and not become stiff and form peaks. The shells will also become brittle over time, and it would not be good to boil the eggs whole, as the shells may crack during boiling. For omelets, basic recipes and scrambled eggs waterglass is an acceptable and viable method of keeping eggs for up to one year. They may last longer if kept in cool conditions, such as a springhouse or refrigerator.

Freezing eggs is always an option if you have an independent method of keeping them frozen in the event of a power outage. First the eggs should be shelled. You can separate the whites from the yolk and store in separate containers. If you are storing yolks separately, you should stabilize them by adding a teaspoon of salt to a cup of twelve yolks. Eggs should be used soon after they are thawed as they will deteriorate rapidly.

It is possible to dehydrate eggs using a home dehydrator. First scramble the raw eggs thoroughly using a blender, then pour this mixture onto teflon sheets on the dehydrator trays to about 1/8 inch level. The dehydrator **must** be able to reach temperatures of 145°, so that any possibility of salmonella bacteria present will be destroyed. Turn the dehydrator to this temperature for the first four hours and then reduce heat to 120° and leave until you have a thin layer of flaked egg crust. This crust can then be placed in the refrigerator for one day to harden the lecithin that is remaining on the egg. Take the hardened egg flakes and blend them in a blender to a fine powder. Vacuum pack this mixture or nitrogen pack it. This will keep the eggs for approximately 12 months. If you cannot vacuum pack you could freeze this mixture. The egg powder can be reconstituted by adding two tablespoons of water to one tablespoon of powdered egg. This will make the equivalent of one egg for scrambled eggs or recipes. Freeze dried or dehydrated powdered eggs can also be purchased in nitrogen packed #10 cans from various distributors.

Sweeteners

Honey

Unpasteurized honey is an excellent choice for food storage as it will store indefinitely and is a natural food. Honey is loaded with enzymes, amino acids and minerals. Because honey is already pre-digested it is easy to assimilate in the body and has many medicinal properties. For these reasons honey is preferable to sugar for a healthy long term food storage program.

There are three types of honey, comb, liquid and crystallized honey. Comb honey is left on the wax combs, just as the bees store it. Liquid honey is spun from the combs and bottled using warming methods. This is the most common form. Crystallized honey is extracted honey which has been bottled unheated. It undergoes a natural process of granulation and will retain its original flavor better than heated honey. Most honey you buy in poly buckets for food storage will crystallize.

If stored in a cool dark place, honey will store indefinitely. It may crystallize over time, but you simply have to warm it to bring it back to the liquid state. To substitute any recipe that calls for sugar replace 1/2 cup of honey for each cup of sugar. For a really sweet taste you can substitute equal parts of honey for equal parts of sugar, but you must reduce another liquid in the recipe by 1/4 cup.

Crude Blackstrap Molasses

This is a highly nutritious food and will store for a long period of time. Molasses was used by the Native Americans as a spring tonic each year because it has so many vitamins and minerals. One gram contains the following minerals and vitamins. Calcium 684 mg, Phosphorus 84 mg., Iron 16.1 mg., Sodium 96 mg., Potassium 2,927 mg., Magnesium 258 mg., Thiamine .11 mg., Riboflavin .19 mg., and Niacin 2 mg. It is also a rich source of most B vitamins. Molasses can be substituted for sugar in most recipes. Use 1/2 cup molasses for one cup sugar. It is best to purchase molasses without preservatives.

Maple Syrup

Maple syrup is another natural sweetening agent that can be stored over a long period of time in a cool dark place. This can be a fairly expensive sweetening agent, but having a small amount in one's food storage program will be welcome on hotcakes or waffles at a later date. You can add water and heat to extend or expand maple syrup.

Water Storage

Water Sources

Water is the most important element in any survival experience. Water is more important than food for the body's existence. The human body can survive for a number of weeks without food, if there is sufficient body fat. One can only live for several days without an adequate supply of fresh water. Dehydration can cause severe mental impairment and eventually death. Obtaining a source of clean drinking water for future survival is an absolute necessity.

The only way to be certain of a fresh, unpolluted source of drinking water is to purchase land and drill a private well, or obtain land with a spring or artesian well already existing. There is a necessity for a clean source of water. This is one of the reasons that leaving the cities is a very strategic element of guaranteeing one's survival in any kind of disaster, natural or man made. At present the source of water in all major metropolitan areas is heavily polluted, not only by human and industrial waste, but by toxic chemicals that are used to attempt to render this water drinkable. Chlorine and fluoride are heavily added to city drinking water, among other chemicals, and these can build up in the body, causing imbalance in the body chemistry. Many known biological diseases are currently being linked to polluted water.

Typical Springhouse

Vent 10" Dia.

Additional Storage and Shelves

Outside Door

Water From Spring

Cheese

Storage Shelf

Milk Cans

Trough

Outlet

Drinking water

Iced Tea

Yogurt

Walls 10-12" thick Made of Stone or Concrete Block

If you are able to purchase land with a private well on it, have the water tested. There are new methods being developed to test your own water, see reference section at the end of the book.

If you have purchased land with a good water source that is gravity fed you are ahead of the game. A surface spring or naturally occurring artesian well can be channeled into a springhouse. The springhouse at the right has a number of purposes, beyond providing a fresh supply of drinking water. An old style springhouse is ideal for keeping things such as milk and butter cool in the summer months. A springhouse can be constructed from simple materials. In fact, this was an essential part of any rural farmhouse only fifty or so years ago.

There are simple ways to collect either rain water or spring water and channel them to a cistern. The cistern acts as a holding tank and distribution area for water

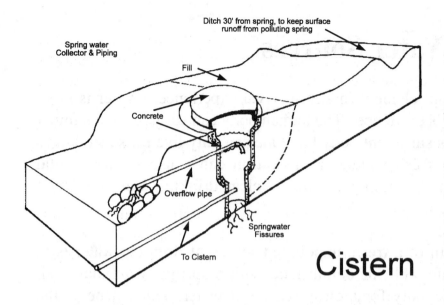

Spring water Collector & Piping

Ditch 30' from spring, to keep surface runoff from polluting spring

Fill

Concrete

Overflow pipe

Springwater Fissures

To Cistern

Cistern

supply. There are many ways to create a cistern arrangement on your property. On this page is just one potential construction. If you have no other source of water than rain water you could still build an adequate cistern and have the rain water funneled into it for water storage. In fact, if you are unable to move to a rural area at this time, you could possibly make some arrangement on your urban property to collect rain water and hold it in case the electricity were turned off and the city water system were unusable.

If you decide that you should have some amount of water held in permanent water storage tanks you need to consider methods of keeping that water purified. There are a number of ways to keep standing water pure for a period of time. Many people use chlorine, but this does have its drawbacks. Chlorine can become deactivated in the presence of amino and ammonia ions. Excessive use of chlorine in water could also be a contributing factor to kidney and bladder diseases. If this is the only method you have of purifying water then use it sparingly, and recycle your water every six months. Using a charcoal filter before drinking chlorine treated water will remove the chlorine. Also boiling the water for 10 minutes removes chlorine.

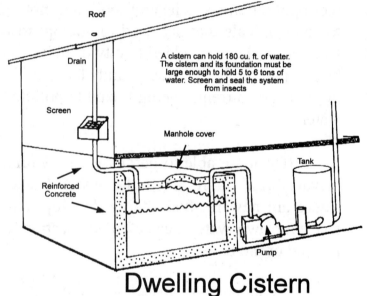

Roof

Drain

Screen

Reinforced Concrete

A cistern can hold 180 cu. ft. of water. The cistern and its foundation must be large enough to hold 5 to 6 tons of water. Screen and seal the system from insects

Manhole cover

Tank

Pump

Dwelling Cistern

Thirty-five percent food grade hydrogen peroxide, H_2O_2, is another method of keeping water pure for an extended period of time. One ounce of H_2O_2 for each fifty gallons of stored water is adequate for six months of storage. After six months it is a good idea to recycle your water. Continue to replace or refresh your water supply as often as practical.

Iodine crystals have been found to be another excellent source of long term water purification. The ratio used is four parts per million. Two ounces of iodine crystals will disinfect 4,000 gallons of water. The simplest way to use iodine to purify a large container of water, 50 gallons, would be to dissolve the iodine crystals in a small quantity of water, (1/4 teaspoon). Take this water with dissolved crystals and add it to another quart container of water, leaving any undissolved crystals in the original container. Add this quart of purified water to the water you are storing. It will be necessary to filter this water through a charcoal filter before drinking to remove the iodine from the water. Excessive iodine is also a potential health problem.

If you are able to purchase land and drill your own well you are fortunate. This is the most ideal method of obtaining pure drinking water. It is important when obtaining land to have it surveyed and all water records for the area provided to you. If it is raw land make sure the seller of the land gives you all pertinent records of water table levels and water rights permit information. Find out how deep the neighboring wells are, and if they have any problem with contamination. The picture to the right gives an approximate understanding of how most water tables are situated and where surface water is in relation to the landscape.

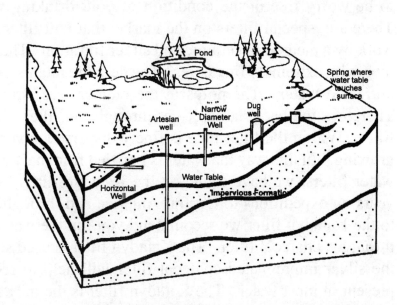

Average Cross Section of a typical Water Table

If you purchase a piece of land with a high water table you could potentially put in your own sand point well. A sand point is a special fitting at the end of a well pipe. It looks like a conical sieve. A sand point is easily created by purchasing some simple tools. Depending upon how close to the surface a steady source of water is, you can put in your own pipe (well casing) and attach a sand point to the end of the pipe. The well will be adequate in areas of high surface water year round. This is practical to a depth of approximately thirty feet, but if the source of water is deeper, you should consider a drilled well. Generally, wells under fifty feet can go dry in the event of an extended drought, so it is advisable to go as deep as you possibly can afford to within 100 feet.

It would be ideal if you could purchase a piece of property with a creek or stream running through it. But, do not assume that because this water runs through your property you have property rights to it. Each state is different in how it treats its water rights. For example, a creek running through a property in Montana belongs to the state of Montana. The state owns the water and the creek bed. You must obtain a special water rights permit depending upon how you want to access or use the water. Check with your local county conservation district and water rights district when purchasing land to determine what the local laws are in this regard.

Methods of Purification

Regardless of your water source it is practical to have some source of water purification on hand in the event that your water does become polluted, or you simply want to be worry free of the condition of your drinking water. There are special filters on the market that will filter out most harmful bacteria. These work by a method of ceramic and silver filtration. The water is forced through a ceramic tube with extremely fine pores. The ceramic retains all suspended matter and bacteria in untreated water. The pores in the element are smaller in size than normal bacteria. Therefore the bacteria can't get through the filter. The bacteria is then caught in the filter. Within the filter tube is finely dispersed silver which prevents the bacteria from growing. In this way the water is purified from bacterial contamination. One of the best water filters, we have found, is the Katadyn filter. We have used this filter for many years on expeditions to Central America and throughout the United States. In addition to the Katadyn filter we recommend you run the water coming out of the Katadyn filter through a charcoal filter. The Katadyn filter is used strictly for bacterial removal. Using the silver impregnated charcoal filter will help to reduce the chemicals and bad taste present in most water. The Katadyn filter is the only filter currently recommended and used by the International Red Cross.

Beyond the water purifiers mentioned previously that use a ceramic filter, you can also use carbon filters that attach directly to your water spigot. These carbon filters will remove a broad spectrum of organic compounds, including pesticides and herbicides, trihalomethanes and many other toxic wastes. They will also remove the chlorine and iodine that you may have used for long term storage. It is best to purchase several carbon filters, as they can wear out with continued use and should be replaced periodically.

The simplest method of purifying water is to boil it for at least five minutes in a rapid boil. To improve the taste of boiled water simply pour it back and forth in a couple of drinking glasses several times to reoxygenate the water.

It is necessary to have a hand pump on a well if you want to insure water without the use of electricity. Most of the hand pump apparatus is installed inside the well, i.e.

cylinder, drop pipe, suction rod, etc.   The only thing attached to the casing is the pumping mechanism faucet, and that requires some of the casing to protrude above the surface. This should be a consideration when you are having your well drilled or evaluated. You can have an electric pump installed within the well, and have a hand pump attached to the well casing. In this way you have pumped water either with or without electricity.

It would be wise to have extra water stored in barrels and drums in case the water table were to become contaminated or a drought situation occur. Fifty gallon drums are available for water storage. Use the above methods of water purification, such as chlorine, H_2O_2 or iodine crystals to keep this water pure for long term storage. This water should be checked every six months for bacteria growth. Replace if you are uncertain as to the purity of your water.

You can't be too careful in obtaining a source of clean drinking water for you and your family. Any research you do in this area, money you spend to purchase filters, land for a sovereign well, and resources to obtain pure water is very well spent. Pure water will be worth more than all the gold in the world if your very survival depends on it.

Reference sources for water: *Home Water Supply: How to Find, Filter, Store and Conserve It*, Garden Way Publishing; *Manual of Individual Water Supply Systems*, Washington D.C. EPA; *Water Supply for Rural Areas and Small Communities*, Edmund G. Wagner.

Medical Supplies

BASIC EMERGENCY MEDICAL SUPPLIES

It is imperative to have certain medical supplies on hand in the event of a short or long term emergency. Access to a doctor or veterinarian could be impossible. In fact, it would be wise to learn to do many medical procedures for your family. If you were in a long term survival situation you would need to maintain the health of your family and animals on your own. There are many books available that specifically address certain emergency medical procedures which we have referenced at the end of this section.

Along with knowledge of basic medical procedures you should store medical emergency supplies. You should also keep on hand any prescription drugs that you are in need of. A working knowledge of homeopathy and herbal medicine would be very beneficial if there were no doctor available to consult. The less dependent you are on a doctor or other professional practitioner , the more sovereign or independent you are. The more knowledge you have, it is likely that you will not only survival any political, economic or natural disaster, but you will survive with little discomfort.

Some Basic Emergency Medical Supplies

Bandages	Tourniquet
Sterile 4 x 4 pad	Flashlight
Gauze (Patch, roll)	Disposable gloves
Band-aids	Aspirin
Triangular bandages	Rubbing Alcohol
Sheets and towels (for dressing)	Vaseline
Elastic, self-adhering	Epsom Salts
Q-tips	Baking Soda
Cotton balls	Hydrogen Peroxide
Roll Cotton	Iodine
Ace Bandages	Table Salt
Gauze Diapers	Cornstarch
Splints	Purex
Scissors	Milk of Magnesia
Tweezers	Pepto-Bismol
Razor Blades	Aloe Vera
Scalpels	Ipecac Syrup (to induce vomiting)
Forceps	Kaopectate (Diarrhea)
Sutures	Paregoric (Pain relief)
Black Silk Thread	Antibiotic Ointment
Surgical Tape	Erogophene Ointment (drawing salve)
Athletic tape	Boric Acid Crystals (Eye wash)
Tongue depressors	Murine (Eye Wash)
Water Bottle	Oil of Cloves (toothache)
Bed pan	Olive Oil
Enema equipment	Cayenne Pepper
Thermometers (oral & rectal)	Ammonia Capsules (Smelling salts)
Ice pack	Antiseptic Soap
Measuring cup and spoons	Tincture of Green Soap
Eyedropper	Snake Bite Kit
Eye glass (to wash eyes)	Castor Oil

Homeopathic First Aid *	Herbs
Antimonium Tararicum	Aloe
Apis Mellifica	Arnica
Aconitum Napellus	Bayberry
Arnica	Black Cohosh
Arsenicum Album	Blessed Thistle
Belladonna	Burdock
Bryonia	Chamomile
Calcerea Fluorica	Cayenne
Calendula Officinalis	Chaparral
Carbo Vegetabilis	Comfrey
Carbolicum Acidum	Dandelion
Cicuta Virosa	Echenacia
Crotalus Horridus	Fennel
Causticum	Garlic
Cantharis	Goldenseal
Chamomilla	Ginger
Cinchona Officinalis	Ginsing
Euphrasia	Licorice
Ferrum Phosphoric	Mullein
Gelsemium	Nettle
Glonionum	Oatstraw
Hypericum	Parsley
Ignatia	Peppermint
Ipecacuanha	Red Clover
Lachesis	Rose Hips
Ledum	Sage
Laurocerasus	Skullcap
Magnesia Phosphirca	Slippery Elm
Mercurius	Tansy
Natrum Suphuricum	Uva Ursi
Nux Mochata	Willow Bark
Nux Vomica	Witch Hazel
Oxalicum Acidum	Yarrow
Phosphorous	
Phytolacca	
Pulsatilla	
Rhus Toxicodendron	
Ruta Graveolens	
Silicia	
Symphytum	
Tarentula Cubensis	
Utica Urens	
Veratrum Album	
Vipera	
Zincum Metallicum	

* Homeopathic First Aid Kits are available. Check supplier section at end of book.

Some good reference sources for first aid medical procedures are: _Emergency Medical Treatment: Adults_ by Stephen Vogel; _Emergency Medical Treatment: Children_ by Stephen Vogel; and _The SAS Survival Handbook_ by John Wiseman; _Where There is No Doctor_ by David Werner; _Where There is No Dentist_ by Murray Dickson.; _Homeopathic First Aid Manual_ by M. Moore; _Homeopathic Medicine For Women_, by Dr. Trevor Smith; _Homeopathy: and Medicine of the New Man_ by George Vitkoulkas

VITAMINS AND MINERALS

If you are currently taking any vitamin or mineral supplements you may want to check with the manufacturer to determine the storage life of these items. Once you have determined what you want to store it would be best to store them in a cool, dry and dark place for the longest storage life. Most multi-vitamin and mineral manufacturers we consulted say their product has full potency up to 3 years. At the end of three years it does not mean you need to discard them, it merely means that they are less potent.

SPIRULINA

Spirulina is a natural source of minerals, vitamins, amino acids and essential proteins. It also has chlorophyll which is an excellent blood purifier.

The vitamin breakdown of spirulina is a natural balanced state of Biotin, B12, D-Ca-Pantothenate, Folic Acid, Inositol, Nicotinic Acid, B1, B2, B6 and Vitamin E. The mineral content is a balance of calcium, phosphorous, iron, sodium, potassium, chloride, magnesium, manganese and zinc. Spirulina contains seven essential amino acids, isoleucine, leucine, methionine, phenylaline, threonine, tryptophan and valine, and ten non-essential amino acids.

Spirulina is such a high source of protein that it is a complete food in itself. It has been suggested that if you had no other food source you could sustain your life simply by ingesting spirulina daily. One of our staff tried it for ten days and maintained their normal energy level. Spirulina will store for several years if kept in a cool, dry and dark place. If you have no other source of vitamins and minerals this would be an excellent way to supplement your diet in hard times.

BARLEY GRASS

This is another excellent source of protein, chlorophyll, amino acids, vitamins and minerals. Since the possibility exists that green leafy vegetables may not be available, this is a must for your food storage plan. Chlorophyll is needed by most all living organisms in the production of sugars. Chlorophyll also helps the liver to manufacture enzymes for the pancreas. Barley Grass has essentially the same qualities as spirulina and has a very alkalizing effect on the body. It will store for several years if kept in a cool, dry and dark place.

HERBS

It would be wise to store your favorite cooking herbs. The shelf life on herbs varies, depending upon how they are stored. They should be kept in a cool, dry and dark place. If possible you should either vacuum pack or nitrogen seal those that you enjoy. It is also wise to keep herbs from exposure to light, as light and heat are what destroys their food value over time. Certain medicinal herbs would be useful to have on hand such as garlic, ginger, Goldenseal, comfrey. or any other medicinal herb that you are familiar with and use regularly. Once these are dried or powdered they can be either vacuum packed or nitrogen packed and stored for many years. The following chart represents some of the historical uses of herbs to relieve simple problems.

PROBLEM	HERBS	PROBLEM	HERBS
Allergies	Bee Pollen, Comfrey	Headache	Wood Betony, Catnip
Anemia	Yellow Dock, Dandelion, Nettle	Hemorrhage	Goldenseal, Capsicum
Asthma	Comfrey, Fenugreek, Lobelia	Infection	Goldenseal, Rose Hips
Back Pain	Garlic & Catnip enema	Nausea	Red Raspberry, Peppermint
Bladder	Marshmallow, Parsley, Dandelion	Nerves	Lobelia, Camomile
Blood Pressure	Black Cohosh, Gotu Kola	Pain	Wood Betony
Blood Purifier	Red Clover, Dandelion, Yellow Dock	Parasites	Garlic, Black Walnut, Wormwood
Boils	Burdock, Chaparral, Dandelion	Pneumonia	Lobelia, Comfrey, Fenugreek
Bronchitis	Comfrey, Goldenseal, Ginger	Poisoning	Lobelia
Bruises	Comfrey Poultice	Shock	Capsicum, Lobelia
Burns	Aloe Vera, Comfrey	Sinus	Comfrey, Goldenseal
Cold	Peppermint, Cayenne, Goldenseal	Sore Throat	Capsicum, Garlic, Comfrey
Colic	Catnip, Mistletoe, Fennel	Sprains	Goldenseal
Constipation	Cascara Sagrada	Swelling	Comfrey, Goldenseal
Coughs	Comfrey, Fenugreek, Elderberry	Swollen Glands	Golden Seal, Mullein, Lobelia
Muscle Cramps	Alfalfa, Black Cohosh	Teeth	Cloves, Lobelia
Menstrual Cramps	Ginger Poultice	Tumors	Red Clover, Chaparral
Diarrhea	Red Raspberry, Slippery Elm	Ulcers	Comfrey
Digestion	Papaya, Peppermint, Dandelion	Vomiting	Red Raspberry, Peppermint
Eyes	Eyebright, Goldenseal, Bayberry	Worms	Black Walnut, Garlic, Wormwood
Fever	Catnip, Yarrow, Garlic	Yeast Infection	Capsicum, Garlic, Goldenseal

Sanitation

Good Sanitation is Critical - Especially After A Disaster

Sanitation is a necessary element in surviving any kind of disaster be it natural or man made. There are a number of supplies to have on hand that will aid you in maintaining sanitary conditions at all times.

Washing hands carefully with soap and a small amount of clean water is an important key to the prevention of intestinal disorders or the spreading of epidemic diseases. It would be wise to have moist towelettes and a waterless soap available, since water may be in short supply. Before handling any food or doing any first aid measures it is imperative to wash your hands. The best method for hand washing would be to purchase or construct a drip water system. A portable shower could serve this purpose. Save the water from cleaning your hands for cleaning your dishes and clothes later.

The disposal of human waste is critical during an emergency. Normal toilet facilities will probably be inoperable without the supply of electricity to pump water. You should also avoid the use of any public toilet facilities during a disaster, as these will most probably be highly contaminated.

If you are confined in a small space you should have available a bucket that can be tightly covered for containing urine. You should also have a bucket available for the disposal of solid waste. The gas fumes from solid waste can be lethal if vented into a small living area. If you are in a shelter the container for solid waste should be vented into the outside air vent and allowed to escape. When you use the bucket for solid waste cover the waste with lime or powdered bleach. Cover with a tight fitting lid if a vent is not possible. Dispose of this as often as possible.

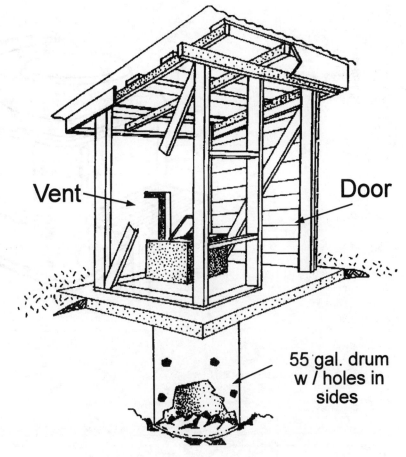

Vent

Door

55 gal. drum
w / holes in
sides

If you are not confined to a shelter dig a latrine outside wherever you are. It should be rectangular, 2' long, 6" wide and as deep as possible (minimum 2 feet). Have available powdered lime or bleach to cover human waste with. When the latrine is filled to within one foot of the surface, cover the entire latrine with dirt and dig a new one.

A conventional outhouse would be the best solution. If you have rural property you would be wise to build an outhouse now and have it available in the event of a sudden emergency. If you live in an urban setting there may be zoning restrictions to this option. This is another reason why you should endeavor to secure some rural property that will be available to you as a long term survival option.

Composting Toilet

A composting toilet could be the solution to some sanitation needs. These toilets use the natural processes of decomposition and evaporation to recycle human wastes. This could be the ideal solution for an underground shelter. Heat, oxygen, moisture and organic material are needed to facilitate the making of compost. This is an excellent way to recycle human waste, without being dependent upon a formal plumbing system or running water via electricity. You are also creating compost which is beneficial to plant growth..

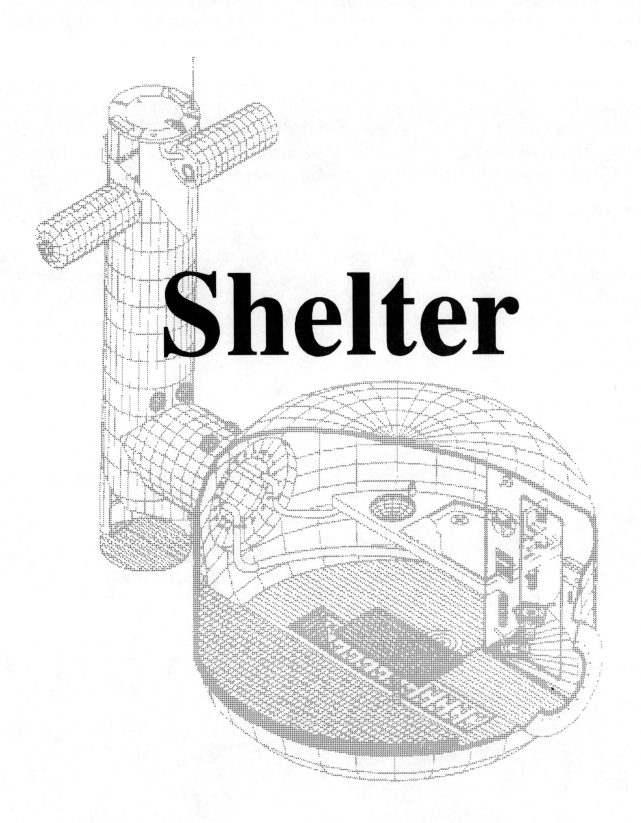

Shelter

Rural Housing

Shelter is a critical consideration in desiring to survive any natural or man made problem that may arise. Our forefathers were aware that natural disasters, such as tornadoes, hurricanes or severe weather conditions, could mandate the need for a special type of shelter so that you could literally ride out the storm. Having an auxiliary shelter could be crucial to your survival in the advent of a nuclear and/or military disaster. Since the 1950s, and the creation of nuclear weapons, fallout shelters have become accepted modes of emergency shelter.

If you are able to obtain rural property that is far from the cities, no matter what kind of problem arises you are ahead of the game. On a few acres you can have a simple dwelling, plus some form of underground shelter, whether it be of a <u>fall out shelter variety</u> or just a <u>simple root cellar</u>. Something that can protect you from nature's stormy weather or a man made disaster such as a nuclear or military catastrophe.

When considering the purchase of rural property there are a number of things to be aware of. First find an area that you are comfortable in and that you feel is far enough away from any major metropolitan area to be safe in the event of any form of disaster. Once you have decided where you would like to settle, begin to look locally for property for sale. You can obtain a local realtor and have them show you everything that is in your price range and area of choice. You should also look on your own for owners who are selling without using a realtor. Many times an "owner contract" or "land contract", where the seller is the lender, can be advantageous to both parties.

Once you find a piece of property you are interested in ask to see the local county extension office water table layouts. You can also get these from the local water right's district. Obtain the actual water rights records for this property. If possible talk to the neighbors. If there is any kind of water running on the property, whether year round or not, check with the water right's district for water permits that have been granted or would need to be granted to make use of surface water. Though it is usually mandatory for a land sale, make sure that the well that is on the property is tested, and that the water is acceptable for drinking purposes. If there is no well on the property check to find out what the depth of the surrounding wells are. Check with the county to find out what the local water testing results are in the area, i.e. whether there is an abundance of iron or any other minerals that would effect the condition of the water.

Make sure all of the zoning information for present and future land use planning is given to you. You need to know what building restrictions might apply to your land

and potential annexing or zoning regulations that are being proposed, if any. Find out if there are any covenants that go with the property that could prohibit you from any future building decisions or land usage.

It is also useful to know what the make-up of the soil is like for any potential underground structures you may want. Whether the area is predominantly clay or loam

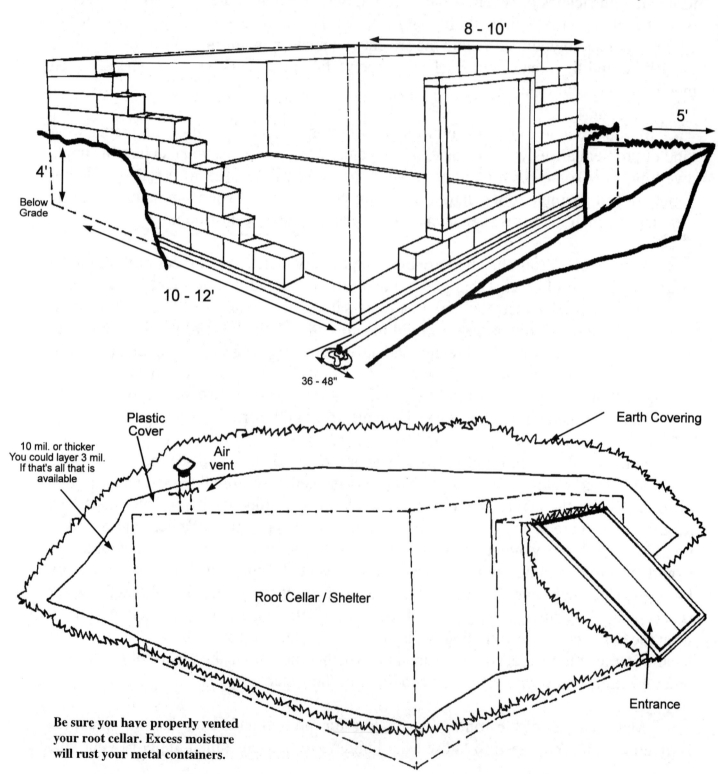

8 - 10'

5'

4'

Below Grade

10 - 12'

36 - 48"

Plastic Cover

10 mil. or thicker
You could layer 3 mil.
If that's all that is
available

Air vent

Earth Covering

Root Cellar / Shelter

Entrance

Be sure you have properly vented your root cellar. Excess moisture will rust your metal containers.

will make a great deal of difference in what the underground water table is like and how it could effect the stability of any underground structure. Before you purchase a piece of property visit the local city hall and find out what the building codes are for your area, and if there are any restrictions on building a fall out shelter, or any other kind of structure.

There are many forms of shelter available that you can either purchase and have placed on your property or buy the materials for and build yourself. A simple root or storm cellar can be built for under $5,000. The more you can do yourself, the less your expenses. There are many plans available in the books listed in the reference section, or you can locate a local architect or builder who can design something for you. We will explore briefly the building of a simple 8' x 12' root cellar so that you can get an idea of what is involved in providing a simple form of auxiliary housing.

View of Root Cellar / Shelter Cross Section

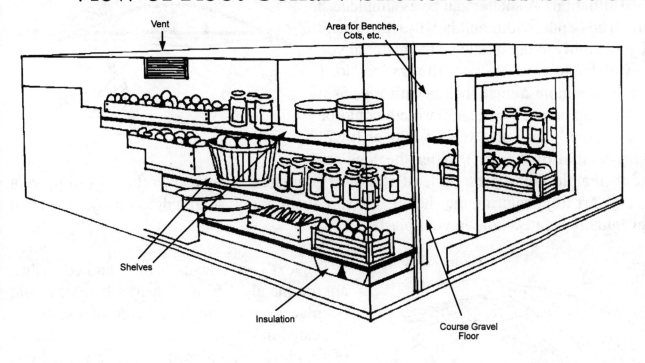

The above picture gives you an idea of what a completed root cellar stocked with food would look like. With this in mind you can determine how much more room you might need to house your family members in the case of any emergency.

To consider building a root cellar you should consult the book <u>Building Small Barns, Sheds & Shelters</u> by Monte Burch, <u>Nuclear War Survival Skills</u> by Cresson H. Kearny, or local contractor for the cellar on the preceding page. If this is all you can afford to build it is still an excellent way to store your food for maximum shelf life and safety. It could also double as an emergency shelter in difficult times.

UNDERGROUND SHELTERS

SIMPLE SHELTERS

Our many years of research and experience has convinced us that safe shelter is a must in a survival situation. The safest place for auxiliary shelter is underground. Underground shelter can withstand catastrophic weather conditions such as tornadoes, hurricanes and electric storms, even potentially an earthquake if you have adequate warning. If properly constructed it would also be the only feasible survival mechanism in the event of a nuclear or biological warfare attack.

TRENCH SHELTER

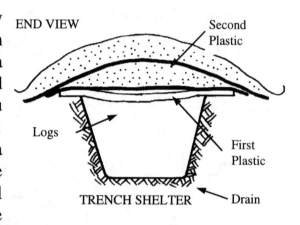

Illustration #1

END VIEW

Second Plastic

Logs

First Plastic

TRENCH SHELTER

Drain

It is not necessary to spend a lot of money in order to have adequate shelter for a short term survival situation. A shelter can be as simple as a trench. The depth, width and height will depend upon your ability to dig it out and the material you have available to cover it over. Illustration No. 1 & 2 show a simple trench shelter with logs as a roof. (A solid core door or similar item could be used if you don't have any logs, as long as it will hold the weight of the dirt). After the logs are placed then a piece of plastic (at least 10 mil or equivalent) is put over the logs to prevent water and dirt from entering the shelter. Be sure there are no sharp edges on your logs that will eventually create a hole in your plastic.

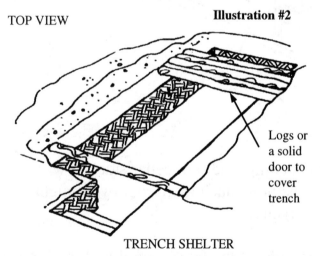

TOP VIEW

Illustration #2

Logs or a solid door to cover trench

TRENCH SHELTER

Next a layer of arched dirt, approximately 1.5' to 2' center height, would be placed over the first layer of plastic as indicated in Illustration No. 1. A second layer of plastic is then placed over this arched dirt and extended at least three feet or more beyond the sides of the shelter. This second piece of plastic is to prevent water from entering the shelter or saturating the ground around the shelter.

Now add another layer of arched dirt approximately 1.5 to 2 feet in height, and taper. The logs or door should be of sufficient strength to support this weight of dirt/roof. The diameter of the logs you use will depend upon the span of the trench you desire. You can build a larger trench if you use larger size logs. On a 3 foot wide trench the logs need to be at least 7 feet long and minimum four inches in diameter. If you want more dirt on top you need to increase the size diameter of logs you use.   If solid core doors are used they are laid perpendicular (crossways) to the trench for strength. One door can only handle up to 2 feet of dirt. More than one door will be necessary for sufficient support of a larger trench with more dirt.

The main point here is that you can have some form of survival shelter without spending a lot of money on an elaborate shelter. This is so simple that with minimal materials anyone can dig a trench and create a shelter. For more details and other ideas of these types of shelter read Nuclear War Survival Skills by C. H. Kearney. See reference section.

TANK SHELTER

One of the easiest quickest and relatively inexpensive ways to have a great shelter is the use of steel and/or fiberglass tanks. The advantages are that they are sturdy when the earth shakes; you don't have to have a hole open for weeks as they can be placed in the ground directly by an experienced excavator operator. Many of the people we consult with throughout the country are using this method of survival shelter. These tanks can be procured as they are being replaced with newer tanks in gas stations or purchased new.

A used tank needs to have entrance and exits installed and be thoroughly cleaned and painted inside. If you are getting a used tank be sure that the contractor who is removing the tank is certified to render it inert.   Most of these tanks have been used for gasoline storage, therefore they could be highly flammable if not properly prepared.

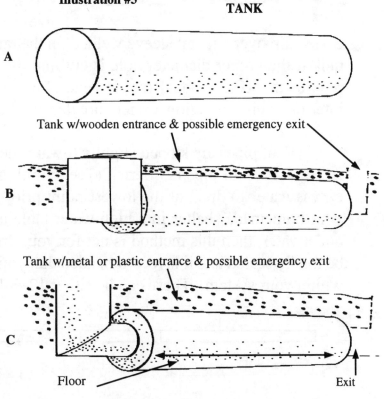

Illustration #3

TANK

Tank w/wooden entrance & possible emergency exit

Tank w/metal or plastic entrance & possible emergency exit

Floor

Exit

On steel tanks a cutting torch is used to cut the desired opening. On a fiberglass tank a power hack saw works wonders. Illustration 3, part A shows a typical tank. Generally they are 8 feet in diameter and anywhere from 16 to 32 feet long. A tank approximately 27 feet long would be adequate for a family of 4 - 5. This would include living space and enough storage for all your food and water for a minimum of one year.

Illustration 3, part B shows a typical wooden type entrance with potential exit on the far end. We always recommend an emergency exit in addition to your main entrance. (Remember a ground hog always has more than one entrance/exit.)

Illustration 3, part C the entrance here is made out of either welded steel, corrugated pipe or the new corrugated plastic pipe now being used in many underground construction projects.

Illustration #4

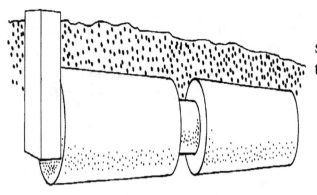

Potential way to hook two tanks together

If you need more room in your underground shelter Illustration 4 is an example of how two tanks can be connected.

Illustration #5

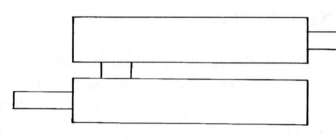

Illustration 5 is another example of how two tanks may be connected together for additional room.

Potential way to hook two tanks together

Illustration #6

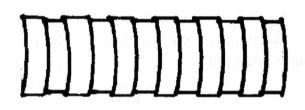

Illustration 6 is a typical corrugated plastic underground pipe used in the construction industry and is great for your underground project. These are ideal for connecting shelters together, used as air vents, and additional storage. Some of the larger sizes come in 32 and 36 inch diameters and will easily slip over a metal sleeve welded on the tank. Or, they could be directly screwed into a tank if the proper diameter hole is cut into the tank to match the pipe. An 8 inch diameter pipe of this type is ideal for air vents. Pipe used as air vents work best if smooth on the interior. This will allow easier curculation of air and reduce condensation buildup.

Vent pipes are sloped slightly toward the shelter to permit water to drain out of them. A Tee section of pipe is inserted (Tee pointing down) just prior to the shelter. This allows excess water to drain at the lowest point prior to entering the shelter. If you are installing your homemade shelter in a high water table area, and any of your airline Tee's would be underwater, then this method is not for you. In this case your airline system would have to be totally sealed and it is recommended that you have a small low volume air circulating fans within your system. These can be either 12-volt electric or hand operated.

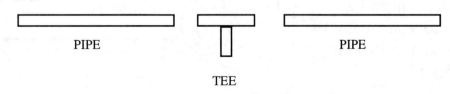

PIPE   TEE   PIPE

ES10 SHELTER

This is a unique, completely self contained shelter. It is totally invisible from the surface when it is installed. If you can afford to protect you and your family with the state-of-the art in survival shelters, this is the model for you.

The ES10 comes with an air filtration system, a toilet, shower and septic system, decontamination devices, communications system and interior lighting. It is approximately 834 cubic feet with headroom from 72 inches to 84 inches. Lighting is supplied by a 10,000 hour fluorescent light located in the bathroom cowling. There are 12-volt 40,000 hour air blowers designed to operate 24 hours per day for up to 45 days. It has twelve 12-volt deep-cycle sealed batteries that are linked together in parallel by heavy duty SAE battery wire.

The command station is designed to resist 500-mph winds and earthquakes which measure 8.5+ on the Richter scale. It is also designed to prevent assaults from people trying to break in. The command station contains a submarine type hatch cover for entry. The shelter can also be provided with 6" national pipe thread outlets for bringing in outside water, a phone line, a power supply, and a 12-volt power cable from a solar panel for recharging the batteries.

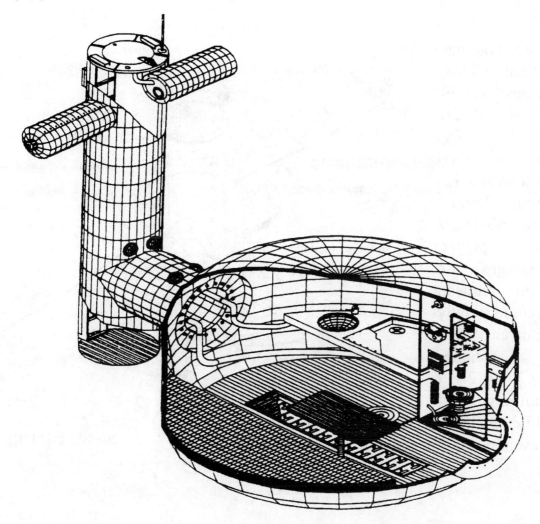

Self-Contained Underground Power Plant

The Self-Contained Underground Power Plant or S.C.U.P.P is a completely self-contained electric power generation plant designed to safely operate as a backup or primary power generation supply in the event of short or long term power collapse. It will resist flying debris in winds up to 200-mph, withstand earthquakes that measure 8.5 on the Richter scale and tolerate 20 psi overpressure from modern weapon detonations.

Another advantage of the S.C.U.P.P is that it allows you to generate power quietly. Therefore, it will not attract attention and provides a more pleasant living environment. The S.C.U.P.P. can be used in conjunction with the ES10 shelter to provide a completely self-contained underground facility.

If you want electric power to run your appliances and water pumping in the event of a catastrophic change in the economy or weather, you will need some kind of generating device. Solar panels and wind generators could be damaged in the event of a natural disaster of high winds or flying debris. If you can afford to be absolutely sure you have power you should consider purchasing the S.C.U.P.P.

This is a diesel engine with a remote start capacity. It can hold up to 280 gallons of fuel. Dif-ferent sizes are available. The S.C.U.P.P. is manufactured with a 12-volt 65 amp charger, 115/230 volt, 60 Hertz single phase power. Custom voltages are available on request. This setup could supply limited power (for recharging shelter batteries, etc.), for 2 - 3 years. Additional fuel supply could extend this time frame even longer.

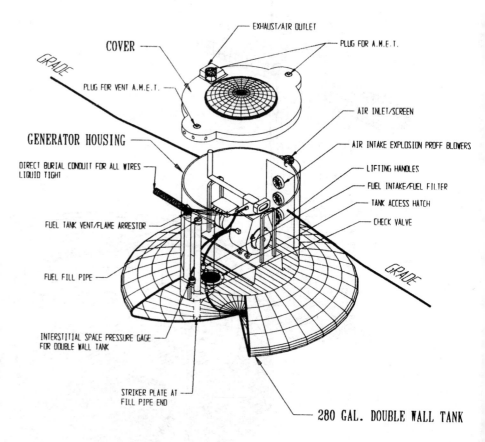

Grains

GRAINS

Wheat is the most basic storage item because it stores well, is highly nutritious and has a myriad of uses. Wheat is the main staple of western civilizations. It can be sprouted, ground, cracked, used for its gluten or even turned into juice. It is highly recommended as storage food if you or a member of your family does not have a wheat allergy. Many individuals have become allergic to wheat as they have been fed highly processed wheat products all of their life that are low in nutrition. If you have been raised on white bread, (where the nutritional value has been stripped from the wheat during processing) you may have developed a wheat allergy. It will take some time to accustom yourself to pure whole wheat products, preferably organically grown wheat. Wheat flour has little nutritional value after about 30 days stored at room temperature. Therefore, it is better to store the whole grain and grind it when needed .

Another valuable grain for food storage is oats. Oats are easily digested, provide good quality protein and are a source of several B vitamins, including inositol. This is a good energy food for active people. Oats also have an alkaline effect on the body. The best source of oats for long term food storage are oat groats and rolled oats.

Millet is another excellent grain for storage. It is still a major food source in Asia and North Africa. Millet has a nutritional profile of 5% fat, 10% protein, .05% sugar, 60% starch, 2.5% fiber, 2.8% minerals, and many of the B vitamins. Millet has many uses in cooking, adding to other grain recipes or rendering to a creamy texture in sauces. Millet is one of the few grains that does not form acid in the body.

Rice is also a valuable grain, and can be a substitute as a staple for those allergic to wheat. Whole grain brown rice is very nutritious, particularly in B vitamins. It has a shorter life span than other grains due to the oil that is retained in the hull. If stored properly in a cool place it will keep for many years. The ideal storage temperature for most grains is 65° or less. It is best to nitrogen pack all grains. In fact, wheat will keep indefinitely if nitrogen packed. Most grains will keep for ten to twenty or more years if properly stored. See following chart.

What Grains and How Much To Store

Food Storage Item	Adult	Teenager	Children
Quantity in Pounds for each Family Member for One year - Range is age/gender sensitive			
Grains, Wheat, Rice, Corn, Barley, Oats, Millet, Rye, etc.	370 - 505	365 - 440	320
Dried Beans, Peas, Lentils, etc.	45	35 - 45	15 - 20
Potatoes	60	65 - 95	25 - 55

BREAD

Bread is a staple food in most cultures. Different breads are created by using different leavening techniques. Leavening makes the bread rise, light and spongy. Leaven is the expansive element in baking bread. The texture of bread is determined by the relationship between the gluten content of the dough and the leavening agent used, if any. A rule of thumb in the potential strength of bread dough is inversely proportional to the amount of leaven. The less leaven you can use and still get a good bread, the better the bread will be, as some people are allergic to yeast products.

There are two types of bread you can make without the necessity of ready made yeast. They are sourdough and unleavened bread. Both breads are desirable if you have no access to commercial yeast or if you have not stored any yeast, or baking powder (non-aluminum).

Sourdough bread is created over a period of several days and creates its own leavening power. There are several methods of making sourdough bread, some of which follow in the recipe section on page 59. To make sourdough starter, combine 1/3 to 1/2 cup of any flour with 1 cup of water. Keep in a warm place and stir daily for one week. The starter needs to be refrigerated when not in use, and will remain active indefinitely as long as it is occasionally fed. Feed by stirring in a tablespoon of flour every week. Save some of the starter every time you make a batch of bread.

Unleavened bread is the most basic bread of all. It contains simple ingredients. This is a tightly textured bread due to the lack of a leavening agent. It can satisfy the desire for bread when only wheat and water are available.

Essene Bread is different from unleavened bread in that it is made with sprouted grain and water. Plain Essene bread has a surprisingly sweet and nutty-rich flavor all its own.

BASIC BREAD MAKING

Homemade bread is much easier than most people imagine. It is also far superior to commercial bread in flavor and texture if done properly. This method will assume that you have no electrical appliances and you are using simple kitchen tools, plus whole wheat flour. See recipes starting on page 59.

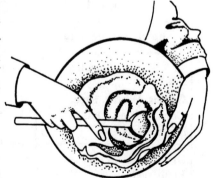

Mixing: Add commercial yeast to moderately warm

water and let it stand for 5 - 10 minutes until bubbles form on surface. This is known as "proofing" and allows you to see whether the yeast is active. The water should be tepid to the touch, as too warm a liquid will kill the yeast. The operating temperatures for yeast are between 100°F and 115°F. You can also add the yeast granules to half of the flour mixture and use warm water in combining your ingredients. Either method is merely one of preference, and should yield the same results. Add the warm liquid ingredients to the flour and mix thoroughly with a wooden spoon or your hands. This helps to properly develop the gluten throughout the dough.

Fold the dough forward on itself and continue to knead the dough.
➔ ➔ ➔

Kneading: Turn the dough out on a lightly

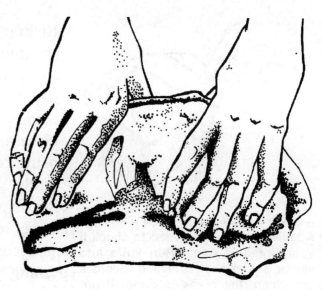

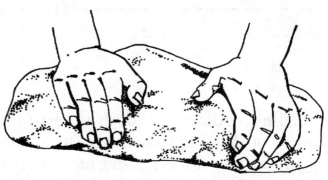

floured surface. Flour your hands also. Curve your fingers over the dough and pull it toward you. Then push it down and away from your with the heel of your hand. Continue this process while you slowly turn the dough sideways in a circular motion. Continue to add flour so that the dough loses its sticky quality. Keep kneading the dough until it is smooth. Kneading can be the key to a good loaf of bread. Too much or too little will effect the quality of the final loaf. Kneading usually takes about eight to ten minutes. Use steady and deliberate strokes, rather than quick and hurried. This will thoroughly mix all of the ingredients and disburse the leavening agent. When the dough begins to feel elastic you are ready to let it rise.

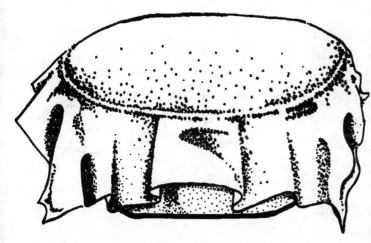

Cover the dough with a slightly damp towel and let rise in a warm (80°) place. 1 1/2 to 2 hrs is required.

Rising: For bread to properly rise it should be placed in an atmosphere of 80°. Rising allows the yeast to grow and give off carbon dioxide which is trapped in the gluten strands and causes the dough to stretch. The rising process is what gives the dough its final texture. Place a lightly dampened cloth over the dough as it is rising to prevent the surface from becoming dry and brittle. When the dough has doubled in bulk it is ready for shaping. Some recipes call for a double kneading and subsequent rising period. This is purely preference and according to the recipe. Punch the dough down by pushing your fist in the center once. Then pull the edges to the center, turn the dough over and place it on a lightly floured surface.

> A knife blade can be used to check if your bread is done. Run knife into center of loaf and remove. If it comes out clean, the bread is done. If not bake some more.

Shaping: Allow the dough to rest for a period of about ten minutes after it has been punched down from the rising process. Roll the bread into a rectangle approximately 12 inches by 8 inches. Seal the seams together and place into whatever baking pan you desire. Prepare the pan by putting some oil or butter on the sides to keep the bread from sticking To aid in browning the crust you can grease the surface of the loaf with butter. Or, brush with egg yolk, sprinkle sesame seeds or rolled oats for a very appealing touch. Cover and let dough rise again until approximately double in size.

Baking: Each recipe will specify the baking time. The average bread is baked at 325° - 350° from 45 to 60 minutes. The oven should be preheated to the appropriate temperature. If you like a brown crust you can begin the baking time with the bread uncovered. After the crust has developed you can put foil over the bread to prevent it from drying out.. Remove yeast breads from baking pans immediately after removing from the oven. Otherwise the crust will be "steamed" in the pan. Place on a wire rack to cool.

> To make buns, roll the dough into round shapes (see drawing) . Place on cookie type sheet and bake. Watch the time, these bake quicker.

52

Use the basic bread recipe for either buns or can bread. Pan Bread is the regular loaf bread we are all familiar with. Can bread is made in #2 1/2, #3 or #10 size tin can. These size cans are those used for most pre-packaged food storage plans. This is handy if you don't have a regular loaf pan. Buns or rolls are simple because you only need a flat surface to bake with. Use basic bread recipe to make buns or rolls on page 59.

Baking Tips

*1. Grind your wheat just before use to retain
    more nutrients and flavor. It is loaded with
    vitamin E plus wheat germ and bran.*

*2. Simple tools are needed, bowl, measuring cup,
    heavy duty spoon (metal or wood).*

*3. Most all breads should be sliced and toasted
    before eating - this aids digestion.*

The following charts will assist you in making bread.➔

BREAD FAULTS AND THEIR CAUSES

PROBLEM	REMEDY
If bread lacks volume, the causes could be	
Too much salt	Reduce salt
Dough chilled during fermentation period	Keep dough warm
Dough not given enough rising time	Increase rising time
Insufficient yeast or yeast is no longer active	Proof yeast prior to adding to dough mixture
Improper mixing and kneading	Check mixing and kneading technique
Oven too hot	Oven temperature correct
Bread pans too small	Use larger pan
If bread volume is too great, the cause could be	
Insufficient amount of salt	Add 1/2 more teaspoon salt
Dough is allowed to rise too long	Only allow dough to rise as long as specified in recipe.
Oven temperature is too cool	Bake bread at 400 - 425°F. for the first 10-15 min. of baking time, then reduce to recipe baking time.
If crust is too dark, the cause could be	
Too much sweetening	Decrease sweetening
Oven too hot	Bake at reduced temperature or check for oven temperature accuracy. Avoid flash heat in beginning stage of baking
Dough had not risen sufficiently	Proof the risen dough by inserting two fingers into dough center; if holes remain without pushing back up again, it has doubled in bulk and is ready.
If crust is too light, the cause could be	
Too little sweetening	Add more sweetening
Oven too cool	Increase oven temperature to proper heat.
Dough is too old	Do not keep dough refrigerated for more than 2 days.
If crust is too thick, the cause could be	
Oven is too cool - requiring a longer baking time that causes thickness in the crust	Increase oven temperature so that bread bakes in allotted time.
Insufficient sugar or honey (sub 1/2 cup honey = 1 cup sugar)	Increase sugar or honey (sub 1/2 cup honey = 1 cup sugar)
If crust is blistered, the cause could be	
Dough has over-risen	Closely watch rising time and proof the dough
Dough hasn't had sufficient rising time	Round and mould dough tightly to avoid air pockets.
Shaping and moulding of loaf is poor	Shape loaf carefully
If the top crust splits or bursts, the cause could be	
Dough is too stiff (too much flour)	Increase liquid in recipe to get proper dough consistency.
Dough was insufficiently risen	Let dough rise until double in bulk, proof dough
Bread pans were placed too close together	Allow at least 3 inches between loaves when baking several loaves.

PROBLEM	REMEDY
If grain is coarse, the cause could be	
Dough was too soft	Use less liquid in recipe
Molding and shaping was poor	Mold dough tighter before placing in pan.
Dough was over-risen	Rise dough less for finer bread even at the cost of volume.
Pan was too large for the quantity of dough	Use a smaller pan that will be 1/4 full of dough.
Oven was too cool	Increase oven temperature to continue proofing in oven
Dough was kneaded excessively	Knead according to directions.
If the bread crumbles and has poor texture the cause could be	
Dough is old	Do not keep dough refrigerated for more than 2 days.
Dough was allowed to rise too long in pan	Do not let bread rise more than 1 inch above top of pan. Shorter rising time results in better bread.
Oven temperature was too cool	Increase oven temperature.
If the bread has holes other than normal fermentation, the cause could be	
Poor molding and shaping of loaf	Round and mold loaf tighter
Excessive greasing of pans or baking containers	Butter or oil pans only lightly and with melted butter if possible.
Excessive amount of dusting flour	Use as little flour as possible when shaping loaf

Shelf Life of Baking Ingredients

Description	Nutritive Storage Life	Storage Life Before Spoilage
Dry Milk, Non-Instant, Low Fat (Nitrogen packed)	4 - 5 yrs.	Indefinitely
Honey	Indefinitely	Indefinitely
Yeast (Vacuum or Nitrogen packed)	1 - 2 years.	3 yrs.
Butter (Vacuum or Nitrogen packed)	5-7 yrs.	10 + yrs.
Salt	Indefinitely	Indefinitely

Definition: Indefinitely = Unclear; vague, Lacking precise limits. American Heritage Dictionary - second edition

Grain Mills

Corona Mill

The Corona Mill is one of least expensive mills on the market. Normally it comes with both steel and stone plates which can be easily interchanged. While this mill currently sells for under $100, it is not precision manufactured and does not give the range of adjustments that the more expensive mills give. Essentially the steel plates are used to do your coarse grinding, such as corn, wheat etc. If a finer grind is needed you can run the coarse grind through again using the stone plates. The Corona Mill is a limited use grain mill. We do not consider suitable for daily use. This mill is not designed for the heavy usage that would be necessary when living exclusively from food storage. It has a small production capacity and requires a lot of energy to grind fine flour. The main advantage of the Corona Mill is that it is light weight and therefore, easier to transport. This mill is good to have on hand as a back-up.

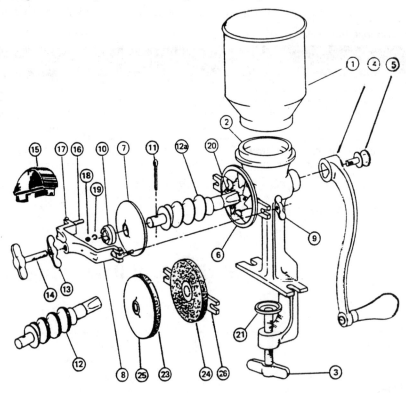

1.	High Hopper	14.	Adjusting Screw
2.	Body	15.	Dust Shield
3.	Clamp Screw	16.	Wing Nut Screw
4.	Crank Handle	17.	Rivet
5.	Crank Handle wing	18.	Ball
6.	Fixed Milling Dice	19.	Ball Spring
7.	Rotating Milling Disc	20.	Screw
8.	Milling Disc Frame	21.	Clamp Screw Washer
9.	Wing Nut	22.	Low Hopper
10.	Milling Disc adjusting Ring	23.	Rotating Stone
11.	Key	24.	Fixed Stone
12.	Feeding Auger	25.	Rotating Stone Casting
12a.	Feeding Auger	26.	Fixed Stone Casting
13.	Retention Wing Nut	27.	Set Milled Metal Grinding Plates
		28.	Washer - for coarse grinding only

Country Living Mill

The Country Living Mill is the most popular hand operated grain mill on the market today. Manufactured exclusively in the U.S., this mill comes with a 20 year warranty and utilizes specially designed steel grinding plates. It runs on industrial ball bearings which should supply a lifetime of service. It is easy to clean and has an infinite amount of adjustment for fineness or coarseness of flour. The mill is very easy to turn by hand, but can be motorized or attached to an exercise bike for ease of operation. This method of operation is done simply by running a V-belt from the mill's flywheel to the motor or device to be used.

In order to process a variety of grains, nuts and beans the County Living Mill is designed to use two different replaceable augers. The wheat auger is standard with the mill and allows a lot of wheat to be fed to the plates. As an option there is a nut and bean auger which can be used to process nuts into nut butters or for grinding up different beans to shorten their cooking times.

The Country Living Mill is the "Cadillac" of hand mills. It requires 30% less energy to grind all grains, beans and seeds into fine flour. It is an attractive mill that blends nicely into any kitchen decor. An optional ceramic flour bin is available to catch the flour as it is ground.

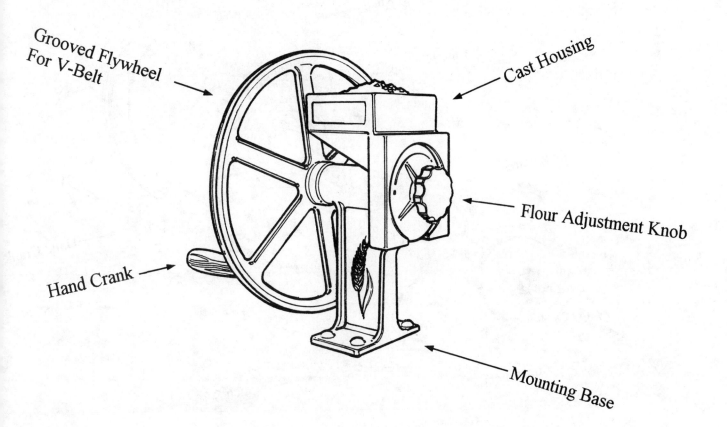

Grooved Flywheel For V-Belt

Cast Housing

Flour Adjustment Knob

Hand Crank

Mounting Base

Diamant

The Diamant grain mill is the "Rolls Royce" of mills. Manufactured in Denmark for fifty years, this mill is designed for heavy duty farm and family use. The mill casing, hopper and mounting plate is forged from heavy duty cast iron. The main spindle rotates on long use main bearings and is a worm type gear fed mechanism. This is ideal for precrushing products such as root crops and other items. The grinding plates themselves are specially cast and hardened and should last for many decades.

To allow ease of turning the mill by hand or motor, the Diamant is filled with a large grooved flywheel. For motorization the mill's flywheel is connected to the motor drive using a V-belt.

Two sets of grinding plates are available with the Diamant. A medium set of plates comes standard with the mill and are suitable for most grinding applications. For chicken and livestock feed, corn or other coarse grains, an optional set of plates can be purchased. Grinding plates are easy to replace by loosening just three hand screws. The Diamant mill will process all manner of grains and beans. This is a mill built to pass on to the next generation.

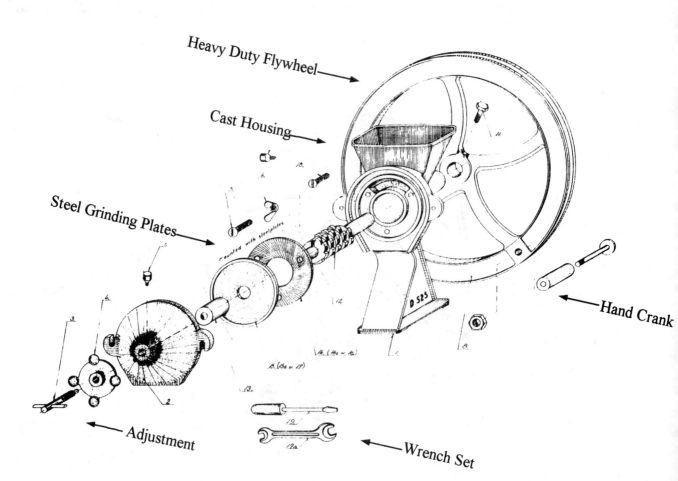

Recipes

Basic Whole Wheat Bread

2 teaspoons active dry yeast
1/2 cup warm water
6 cups whole wheat bread flour
2 1/2 teaspoons salt
2 1/4 cups lukewarm water
(2 tablespoons honey or other sweetener)
(2 tablespoons oil or butter)

Warm your yeast-dissolving cup by rinsing with warm tap water. Measure 1/2 cup warm water into it. If there are directions on yeast package, follow them. The water should be 110°F or warm to touch (not hot or cold). Sprinkle yeast into water while stirring with spoon, being sure each granule is wetted. Completely dissolve yeast.

Sift the flour into its container and measure 6 cups into your large bowl. Measure salt and stir into the flour, making a well in the center. Mix oil and honey, if used, into the 2 1/4 cups water and pour it and the yeast mixture into the well you have made in the flour. Stir the liquid mixture into the flour, beginning in the center and working outward so that you first make a smooth batter, then gradually mix the rest of the flour to make a soft dough. Squeeze with your wet fingers to make sure the dough is evenly mixed; it will be sticky. Flour hands and begin to knead dough. After dough is properly kneaded for 8 - 10 minutes let rise until double in size. Shape into loaf and bake.
Preheat oven to 350° and bake for approximately one hour.

Basic Sourdough Bread

2 cups basic sourdough batter (see Basic Bread Making sourdough starter)
4 cups sifted flour
2 tablespoons honey
1 teaspoon salt
2 tablespoons vegetable oil or shortening

Sift dry ingredients into a bowl, making a well in the center. Add oil to basic batter and mix well. Pour into the well of flour. Add enough flour to make a soft dough for kneading. Knead on a floured board for 10 to 15 minutes. Place in a greased loaf pan. Cover and let rise until doubled in size. Bake at 375° for 1 hour. Makes 1 loaf.

Basic Raisin Bread

1 medium size potato
4 cups water
2 tablespoons butter
2 teaspoons salt
2 tablespoons dry yeast
1 cup warm water
1/2 cup honey
6 cups whole wheat flour
5 1/2 cups unbleached white flour
1 pound raisins (4 cups)
1/2 teaspoon ground cloves
2 teaspoons ground cinnamon

Peel potato and cut into pieces. Cook covered until tender. Mash potato, return it to the water in which it was cooked, add butter salt, and combine. Cool until lukewarm.

Dissolve yeast in 1 cup warm water. Let stand 5 to 10 minutes. Add honey.

Add whole wheat flour to potato mixture, beating until smooth. Mix in the yeast. Beat thoroughly. Cover and let rise for about 1 hour.

Work in unbleached flour to make a soft dough. Stir in raisins, cloves and cinnamon. Knead until smooth on floured board. Put dough in an oiled bowl and turn to oil top. Cover with wet cloth and let rise until double in bulk (about 1 to 1 1/2 hours). Let rise in warm area between 70 - 80°.

Punch down dough, and divide into 3 portions. Place each in an 8 1/2 x 4 1/2 inch greased loaf pan. Cover and let rise again until double.

Preheat oven to 375°F. Bake for 40 minutes.
Yields: 3 loaves

Unleavened Bread

1 2/3 cups water
4 cups whole wheat flour

Put water in a large bowl. Add 3 cups of flour. Stir. Add the last cup of flour gradually, stirring until the batter is too stiff to stir. Knead in remaining amount of flour. Knead about 20 times, until the water and flour are well mixed. Shape into loaf as you knead. Oil a small loaf pan. Place the loaf in the pan. Cover with a damp towel and let rise in a warm place overnight or for approximately 15 - 24 hours. Unleavened breads take longer to rise because they have to develop their own yeast. In the summer rising time could be less, depending upon the temperature. The towel should be kept damp throughout the rising time.

Bake 1 hour at 350°. The crust will be chewy and hard. If the bread did not rise to the top of the loaf pan, bake 30 minutes at 250° and then at 350° until crust is hard. Cool on rack.

Different flours absorb water differently. You may need more or less than 4 cups of flour. Artesian or other well water helps the bread rise.

When making variations of this recipe, always add supplementary ingredients before flour.

Uncle Tom's Whole Wheat Sponge Cake

6 very large eggs, separated
1 cup sugar or 1/2 cup honey
1/2 cup water
1/ teaspoon vanilla
1/2 teaspoon lemon extract
1/4 teaspoon almond extract
1 1/2 cup sifted whole wheat flour
1/4 teaspoon salt
1 teaspoon cream of tartar

Using a small bowl, beat the egg yolks, water, sugar and flavorings for 5 to 7 minutes, until thick and creamy. Transfer mixture to larger bowl. Sift flour and salt together and add to above mixture, gradually beating as you go. In another bowl, beat whites and cream of tartar until stiff. Fold immediately into first mixture. Bake in an ungreased angel tin for 60 to 70 minutes or until top springs back, at 325 to 350°. Invert pan and cool thoroughly before removing. Glaze if desired.

Quick Whole Wheat Chocolate or Carob Cake

3 cups whole wheat flour
6 tablespoon sifted cocoa or carob powder
2 teaspoons baking soda
1 1/2 cups sugar or equivalent honey
1 teaspoon salt
2/3 cups cooking oil
2 tablespoons vinegar
5 teaspoons vanilla
2 cups water

Mix dry ingredients together in bowl. Add remaining ingredients and mix until almost smooth. Bake in a 9 x 13 greased pan at 350° for about 30 minutes. May also be baked in 2 greased and floured 8-inch pans for 20 to 25 minutes.

Crumb Cake

Mix as for pie crust and reserve quantity the size of an egg.
1 cup sugar or equivalent honey
1/2 cup margarine or butter
2 cups whole wheat flour

ADD:
1 cup sour milk
1 tablespoon baking soda
1 beaten egg
1 teaspoon cinnamon
1 teaspoon nutmeg
1 teaspoon cloves
1 cup raisins or other dried fruit chopped

Mix all ingredients together and pour into 9 x 9 greased pan. Sprinkle reserved crumbs over batter in pan. Bake at 350° for 30 to 40 minutes.

Processing
Foods

PRESERVING FRUITS AND VEGETABLES

HOME CANNING

If you are going to preserve fruits and vegetables from your own garden, or fresh produce that you buy, you are going to have to learn to can at home in jars. This is a time honored method of preserving food for several years. If you store your home canned food in a root cellar you could possibly get a longer shelf life. Each fruit and vegetable has its own shelf life, see chart on page 21.

Home canning is not difficult, it merely requires careful attention to cleanliness and following safe procedures in order to avoid future spoilage. This is probably the only method there is of storing pure organic produce. Home canning is very satisfying, particularly when you are preparing the produce from your own garden or the garden of someone you know. It is a fairly inexpensive way of preserving food for future use. You can reuse the canning jars over and over. The initial investment in a waterbath canning container is not expensive, and the few items necessary for easy canning are readily available.

HIGH ACID - PROCESS AT 212°F IN BOILING WATER BATH	LOW ACID PROCESS AT 240°F IN PRESSURE CANNER
Apples, apricot, blueberry, blackberry, cranberry, grapefruit, orange, peach, pear, plum, pineapple, prune, rhubarb, sweet cherry, sour cherry, strawberry and tomato	Asparagus, beans, beets, broccoli, brussel sprouts, carrot, cucumber, cabbage, corn, cauliflower, fig, lima bean, mushrooms, okra, olive, parsnip, pepper, pea, pimento, snap bean, squash, sweet potato, turnip and white potato

WATER BATH CANNING

First of all clear some space in your kitchen and organize the various canning essentials in one area. To water bath either fruit or vegetables you will need a water bath container. These are readily available at any survival or hardware store. You will also need hot pads, a jar lifter, canning funnel, and last but not least, canning jars with appropriate lids. You can choose either pint or quarts jars as you prefer for storage space.

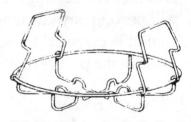

Rack for boiling-water-bath canning. Use in a pot with a lid.

Begin by placing the jars empty and upside down in the water bath canner and add about one inch of water.

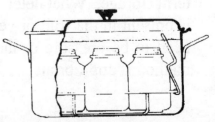

Boiling-water bath. Cutaway shows jars in position.

Put the lid on the waterbath and bring to a boil. Allow to boil mildly for approximately fifteen minutes. This will sterilize the jars and render them warm for accepting hot liquids. Also place the sealing lids into the boiling water to sterilize..

Prepare your fruits or vegetables according to directions for either cold pack or hot pack. Raw or cold pack means that the food is uncooked and placed directly into the warm canning jar. Only hot liquid is added. Hot Pack refers to food that is precooked to some degree before processing. Though many foods can be either raw or hot packed, it is best to check the chart on page 68 to determine which method is optimal for each food.

Once you have determined how to prepare your fruit or vegetable, place them into the jars, leaving at least one half inch head room at the top. The head room allows for expansion during the heating process. Any liquid poured into the jar should come short of the top by at least one half inch. Take a clean towel and wipe the rim of the jars thoroughly before placing the sealing lid on. Apply the ring, tighten firmly, and then turn back one quarter turn to allow for possible expansion.

Place the jars into the waterbath canner. Add water to canner so that it covers the jars by at least one inch. Place the lid on the canner and turn the heat to high and bring the water to a boil. Once the water is at a rolling boil turn the heat down to allow for a steady boiling temperature. Check the chart on page 68 for the processing time.

Once the processing time is up, turn the heat off and crack the lid, allowing time for the heat/cold to equalize. Remove lid when all steam has escaped. Use the jar lifter to remove the jars from the hot water. Place jars in an area free from drafts and keep them at least half an inch apart. Don't allow the hot jars to touch each other, as this will prevent even cooling. Place a thick towel over all the jars so that they cool slowly. This will prevent any cracking of jars and allow for a tight seal on the lids. When thoroughly cool, it is essential to place the name and date of the food on the top or side of the jar to assist in the proper rotation of your food storage.

PRESSURE CANNING

Many fruits and vegetables need to be pressure canned for maximum safety in long term storage. What determines the need to water bath or pressure can is how much acid is present in the fruit or vegetable. High acid foods can be water bathed, low acid foods need to be pressure canned. The following chart, pages 68 - 70, will indicate which method is appropriate.

DIAL-GAUGE PRESSURE CANNING

This is the recommended method of pressure canning, as the amount of pressure can be easily determined and regulated. The dial gauge registers the pounds of steam pressure being produced in the canner. The gauge should be checked each year for accuracy. Most Cooperative Extension Agencies at the county level can check you dial gauge for you.

Prepare your food by either hot pack or raw pack method as you prefer. The chart on page 69 will indicate the length of time and pounds of pressure to use for each food. Place each jar upright in the canner. There should be a special basket with the canner that will keep the jars from touching each other or touching the bottom of the canner.

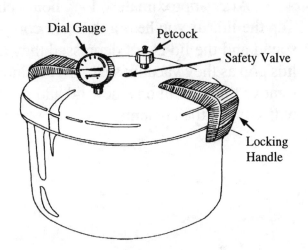

Pour three quarts of hot water into the canner over the jars. Put the lid of the pressure canner on and make sure that it is securely fastened according to the directions with the canner. If it has locks, be sure they are securely locked.

Pressure Canner

Rubber gasket canners - The lid may have arrows pointing to a closed position, and the handles may need to be centered over each other.

Metal to Metal canner. Screw down the thumb-screws, always tightening two opposite knobs at the same time. This will ensure that they are sealed evenly. Be sure control valve is open.

It is important that your escape valve is open and not blocked by anything. Set the burner to the highest heat possible. When steam flows freely from the vent pipe allow this steam to rise for approximately 2-3 minutes. This will allow extra air to escape the canner. After 2-3 minutes place the pressure cap or regulator over the vent pipe. This will allow the pressure to build in the canner. The pressure valve gauge should begin to rise. When the pressure has risen to the desired pounds of pressure begin to count the time of canning according to the chart on page 69. You can at this time turn down the heat so that it is constant and remains constant during the steaming process.

It is best to use a timer and remain in the cooking area during the processing period. Adjust the heat to meet the canning specifications. If the heat is too low or too high, the cooking pressure will vary, causing damage to the product being canned. Always follow the manufacturer's recommendations for time and pressure. If these are not followed the produce will spoil which can cause botulism. STAY ALERT!

Once the proper time has elapsed remove the pressure canner from the heat source. Do this very carefully without jarring the canner or removing the lid. NEVER REMOVE THE LID OF A PRESSURE CANNER UNTIL THE PRESSURE HAS AGAIN REACHED ZERO POUNDS. Carefully running cold water over the canner will speed up the cooling down process. Allow the pressure canner to thoroughly cool for at least 15 minutes before removing the lid. When removing the jars from the canner, place them in a draft free area with a thick towel over them to prevent them from cooling too rapidly.

After approximately 1 - 2 hours check the lids on the jars to see if they are sealed. Tap the lid. If you hear a dull and compact sound they are sealed. If you hear a hollow sound and the lid is not depressed they have not sealed properly. You can also hear the lids pop as they vacuum seal. If you find some that have not sealed properly immediately remove the lid. Put on a new lid and put them through the water bath process again. This will salvage the contents.

WATER BATH CANNING AT 212°F (Boiling) (Processing Time in Minutes)			
FRUIT	**TYPE PACK**	**PINTS (Minutes)**	**QUARTS (Minutes)**
Apples	Hot	20	20
Applesauce	Hot	20	20
Apricots	Raw	20	20
Apricots	Hot	20	25
Berries	Raw	15	20
Berries	Hot	10	15
Cherries	Raw	20	25
Cherries	Hot	10	15
Currants	Raw	15	20
Figs	Hot	85	90
Grapes	Hot	15	20
Grapes	Raw	20	25
Grapefruit	Raw	10	10
Guavas	Hot	15	20
Loquats	Hot	15	20
Nectarines	Raw	25	30
Peaches	Raw	25	30
Peaches	Hot	20	25
Pears	Hot	20	25
Persimmons	Hot	15	20
Pineapple	Hot	15	20
Plums	Hot	20	25
Rhubarb	Hot	15	15
Strawberries	Hot	10	15
Tomatoes	Hot	35	45

HOT PACK: Hot pack refers to foods that are precooked to some degree, then put into jars warm for processing. This makes for more compact packing. A hot pack sometimes requires less cooking time, since the food is already partially cooked.

RAW PACK: This refers to food that is packed uncooked. The raw food is packed into the jars and hot liquid is added, then the processing begins.

PRESSURE CANNING AT 10 Lb. PRESSURE			
VEGETABLE	**TYPE PACK**	**PINTS (Minutes)**	**QUARTS (Minutes)**
Artichokes	Hot	25	30
Asparagus	Raw	25	30
Beans, Dried	Hot	75	90
Beans, Lima	Raw	40	50
Beans, Green	Raw	20	25
Beets	Hot	30	35
Broccoli	Hot	25	30
Brussel Sprouts	Hot	25	30
Cabbage	Hot	25	30
Carrots	Raw	25	30
Cauliflower	Hot	25	30
Celery	Hot	30	35
Corn, Cream style	Raw	95	100
Corn, Whole	Raw	55	85
Eggplant	Hot	30	40
Mushrooms	Hot	45	50
Onions	Hot	25	30
Peas, green	Raw	40	40
Beans, New	Raw	20	25
Peppers, sweet	Hot	50	60
Potatoes	Hot	35	40
Pumpkins	Hot	55	90
Salsify	Hot	30	35
Soybeans	Hot	55	65
Spinach	Hot	70	90
Sweet potatoes	Hot	55	90
Turnips, Parsnips	Hot	25	30
Vegetable Soup	Hot	60	75
Zucchini	Raw	30	40
Summer squash	Hot	30	40

PRESSURE CANNING MEAT AT 10 Lbs. PRESSURE
(Processing Time in Minutes)

MEAT	TYPE PACK	PINTS (Minutes)	QUARTS (Minutes)
Beef	Hot	75	90
Veal	Hot	75	90
Lamb	Hot	75	90
Pork	Hot	75	90
Sausage	Hot	75	90
Poultry	Hot, With Bone	65	75
Poultry	Hot, Without Bone	75	90
Rabbit	Hot	65	90
Corned Beef	Raw	75	90
Fish	Hot	75	90

SIGNS OF SPOILAGE

GLASS JARS

1. A jar that is soiled or moldy on the outside indicates that food has seeped out during storage, which means that air, bacteria, yeasts, and molds could have seeped in.
2. A significant change in color, most notably a much darker color, can mean spoilage. Some brown, black or gray discoloring may be due to minerals in the water or in the cooking utensils; while it may detract from the looks of the food, there is no harm done otherwise.
3. A change in texture, especially if the food feels slimy, is a sure sign that the food isn't fit to eat.
4. Mold in the food or inside the lid - sometimes nothing more than little flecks - is not a good sign.
5. Small bubbles in the liquid or a release of gas, however slight, when you open the can means foul play. Sometimes you get a strong message: liquid actually spurts out when you release the seal; other times the gas is more subtle.
6. Lids can be removed just by finger pressure.

TIN CANS

1. Bulging ends or liquid leaking from the seam, where the lid meets the can, spells trouble.

°F 250		°C 121	BACTERIA CONTROL TEMPERATURE CHART
240		116	Canning temperatures for low-acid vegetables, meat, and poultry in pressure canning.
212		100	Canning temperatures for fruits, tomatoes, and pickles in water-bath container.
165		74	Cooking temperatures destroy most bacteria. Time required to kill bacteria decreases as temperature is increased.
140		60	Warming temperatures prevent growth but allow survival of some bacteria.
120		49	Some bacteria growth may occur. Many bacteria survive.
60		15	DANGER ZONE - Temperatures in this zone allow rapid growth of bacteria and production of toxins by some bacteria.
40		4.5	Some growth of food poisoning bacteria may occur. (Do not store meats, poultry, or seafood for more than a week in the refrigerator).
32		0	Cold temperatures permit slow growth of some bacteria that cause spoilage.
0		-18	Freezing temperatures stop growth of bacteria, but may allow bacteria to survive. (Do not store food above 10°F for more than a few weeks.)

Smoking Meat

The two methods of smoking meat are cold smoking and hot smoking.

Cold Smoking: This refers to a slow, smoulder smoke that seldom gets above 70° - 90°F. The meat is never cooked during cold smoking because the smoke never becomes hot enough.

Hot Smoking: This is basically cooking with very hot smoke. Since the meat has been cooked it must be either consumed, canned or frozen immediately afterward.

Smoking meat is a simple process that only requires a fire pit and a smoke chamber where the meat is actually smoked. The meat to be smoked is always put through the curing process before smoking, see page 75. A smoke chamber can be easily created from simple materials. One can also turn an old refrigerator into a smokehouse, or a fifty-five gallon drum.

The Fire Pit - The fire pit is set into the ground 2 to 2 1/2 feet deep. This could be an old kettle, a simple box or any type of enclosure that would hold a fire. A hole in the ground lined with rocks will also do. The pit must have a top as this will act as a damper to help regulate the draft and to control the amount of fire in the pit. A metal cover would be ideal, but a piece of sheet metal will work.

The Smoke Chamber - The chamber is where the meat is actually smoked. It should be large enough to accommodate the amount of meat being smoked. Be sure

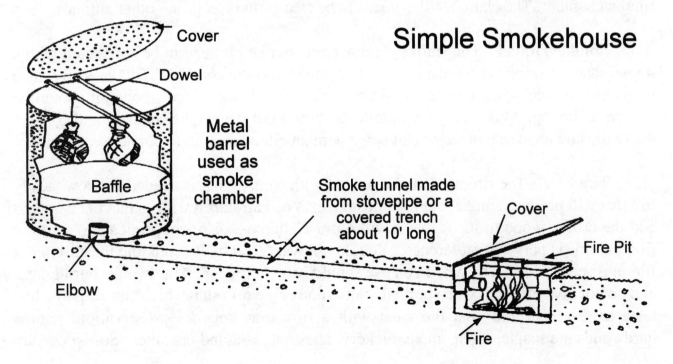

Simple Smokehouse

Cover

Dowel

Metal barrel used as smoke chamber

Baffle

Smoke tunnel made from stovepipe or a covered trench about 10' long

Cover

Fire Pit

Elbow

Fire

that the chamber is clean. There should be no paint or fresh painted enamel inside.

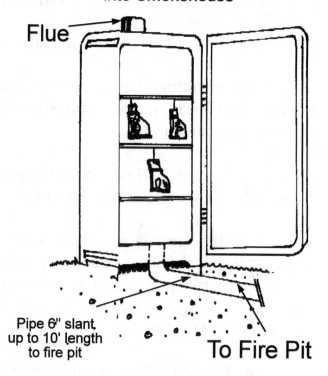

Old Refrigerator converted into Smokehouse

Flue

Pipe 6" slant up to 10' length to fire pit

To Fire Pit

The chamber must have a method to control the amount of smoke that will escape. This can be a suspended damper with holes drilled in it (see picture on previous page). There needs to be fresh smoke constantly rising around and past the meat. The chamber must also have a top that can be opened and closed in a controlled way to act as a damper for the draft.

The meat needs to be suspended in the chamber while being smoked. Dowels are fine to use as crosspieces. Twine, wire, S-hooks or similar means may be used to suspend the meat from the crosspieces. You can use wire mesh shelves also. They should be installed to provide for easy removal for cleaning. Stay away from galvanized wire, brass or copper, as these give off oxides or chemicals that are harmful to the meat and the one who consumes it.

The base of the smoke chamber should ideally be elevated above the top of the fire pit and to the side about ten feet away. This facilitates the draft from the fire pit to the smoke chamber. The chamber also needs to be free from insects and other animals.

Smoke Tunnel - The smoke chamber and smoke pit need to be connected with a tunnel that the smoke can escape from the fire pit into the chamber This is easily done by making a hole, approximately 6" in diameter, in the side of the smoke pit about one foot from the top. Make a similar hole in the bottom of the smoke chamber and connect the two. You can use a piece of stovepipe with an elbow section to connect each end.

The Fire - The fire needs to be tended with care. What is needed is a low steady fire that will produce smoke, but not hot smoke. You can start it with a charcoal base and add the proper wood to it. A purist will not use charcoal or petrochemicals to start the fire, but this is personal preference. You do not want to actually cook the meat, so a hot fire must be avoided. The wood you use should be a hardwood. Hardwoods burn longer and do not give off pitch when burned. Softwoods give off pitch which can impart a bad taste to the meat and coat the meat with a film that impedes preservation. Some hardwoods are maple, birch, apple, hickory, chestnut, ash, and oak, etc. Softwoods are pine, cedar, spruce, hemlock, cottonwood and balsam. Some people have also used dried corn cobs with success. The wood should be cut into small pieces or shavings. Use green twigs or green leaves from hardwood trees to smoulder and create gentle smoke.

Smoke - It is important that the meat in the chamber be properly exposed to the smoke; otherwise the flavor is not evenly distributed and the meat not properly preserved. No meat should touch another piece of meat nor the sides of the chamber. To allow the smoke to escape the chamber you can punch holes in the top of the chamber. You can also create a baffle under the meat to evenly distribute the smoke throughout the chamber.

Notes

Curing

Curing is the process of preserving meat for future needs primarily with the use of salt. A by-product of the curing process is the added flavor that curing imparts. In most instances meat to be smoked must be cured first.

One of the most important things to keep in mind when curing meat is that all meats have a high percentage of water which must be removed to prevent spoilage. The application of salt is what extracts the water. Salt also produces an antibacterial action which is what preserves the meat.

The curing process takes times. The larger the pieces of meat, the longer the time required. Use coarse table salt. Sugar is added to counteract color loss, prevent severe dehydration of the meat and to sweeten the flavor. Maple syrup or honey can also be used.

Salt peter can also be added to the curing process as a preservative, but we do not recommend it in this book. Salt peter is part of the potassium or sodium nitrate family, and therefore, adds nitrates to the finished product. Nitrates are known to be carcinogens.

A dry cure is when the curing ingredients are mixed thoroughly and used on the meat in a dry state. A wet cure is when the dry ingredients are mixed with pure water to create a brine or sweet pickle. The brine cure can take a little longer, but is less salty.

Curing Process

If you are dealing with an animal that has just been killed you need to bleed it completely. Blood spoils meat faster than anything else. Before curing, the animal should be chilled for several days and hung where no other animals have access to it. Chilling slows down the bacterial and enzyme action which causes the meat to spoil. The meat must be chilled thoroughly, right through to the bone. This should be done as close to 32°F as possible.

Polybucket can be used as a curing container

Everything must be very clean and sanitary during the entire curing process. For dry or wet cures you need the following:

A crock or hard-wood barrel to do the curing in if you use the sweet pickle (wet) method, probably holding five or ten gallons minimum. A poly-bucket works fine too.

A wooden box with holes in the bottom to cure the meat in if you are using the dry cure.

A basic recipe for curing would be 8 pounds of salt and 2 pounds of sugar for a dry cure. If you want to do a brine or wet cure you add 4.5 gallons of water to the salt and sugar. You may add any spices that you feel would enhance the flavor of the meat.

For a dry cure each piece of meat should be thoroughly rubbed with the dry mixture. Don't worry about using too much. Put a good layer of the curing mixture on the bottom of the box or container you are using. Place the largest pieces of meat at the bottom, skin- side down. Continue to layer the curing mixture and the meat until all the meat is covered. The meat will remain in this container for four days. The meat is then removed from the container, reworked with the dry mixture, and again repacked. Here it is left for two days. If the weather is cold the curing time is lengthened. If the weather is hot the time is shortened.

To prepare a shoulder of ham for smoking, use the following method. Trim off excess fat and round or shape the meat as needed. Keep in mind that this item will be hung up for smoking later. The excess trimmings can be used in the liver pudding recipe on page 79. Cut open a large paper bag and lay flat. Cover the bag with your curing mixture. A recommended mixture is one pint of coarse table salt, two Tbs. of pepper and two Tbs. of brown sugar. Lay meat with skin side down on curing mixture. Cover meat with mixture. Work into all crevices, especially around the end of the bone. Wrap the meat in the paper bag. Wrap this in a muslin or cotton bag. Grains such as rice and beans are marketed in these bags. The bag must be securely fastened around meat the and sewn shut. Wrap again with heavy twine or strong rope, and hang from hooks in smoking chamber.

For the brine, cure dissolve the salt and sugar into cold water. Make certain that the water is pure, even if you have to boil it to sterilize it. The liquid brine should fill your curing container to about one third full. Insert the meat into the brine, ensuring that each piece is surrounded by solution and properly covered. Place a plate on top of the meat or any kind of weight that will keep it fully immersed. Keep this in the solution for five to six days. The meat is then removed, repacked and left to cure for another week. By this time the process should be completed.

Fish

Fish is delicate in terms of shelf life or storage. It must be processed quickly or eaten soon after catching. It is important to keep fresh fish as cool as possible up to processing time. Fish can be cured by either a dry or a brine curing method. To cure fish clean thoroughly and remove the head, tail and backbone. Inspect to be sure that all blood and foreign matter is removed. Drain for 15 minutes and wash in a mild salt solution of 1 cup of salt to one gallon of pure water.

If you are dry curing layer fish in a container using salt in between each layer. Warm weather requires two to three days of curing. In cool weather you can leave the dry cure for up to a week. The size and thickness of the fish will determine the total curing time. Once the salt curing is done the fish should be removed from the container. Wash to remove all residue of salt. Air dry on a protected rack in the shade. Turn often. You may dehydrate if desired. The fish is done when no dent is left when squeezed between thumb and forefinger. Wrap in wax paper and store in a cool dry place. If sufficiently dry, fish cured in this way may store for up to two years.

Brine curing is essentially the same as the dry cure except that you add water to the recipe. 1 1/2 cups of salt to 1 gallon of pure water. Fill a crock with layered fish and salt mixture. Add water and cure for one week. Remove from solution and clean fish again in pure water. Put fish back into brine solution for up to three months. Maximum storage time for brined fish is about 9 - 10 months.

To smoke fish that have been cured in a brine solution, or any of the above methods, remove fish from curing solution and air dry thoroughly. Place fish in a smokehouse after all salt has been removed. See the instructions for smoking on page 72.

The longer fish is smoked, the longer it may be stored. Fish tends to spoil easily, once the smoking process has begun, therefore it should be completed without interruption.

To dry fish, you can hang them on a rack in the sun. Minnows and small fish can be dried whole after they have been cleaned. Larger fish should have the backbone cracked before they are hung to dry, bones and all. You can debone fish if you prefer and hang the fillets up to dry. When the fish are leathery to the touch, at least one week, they should be sufficiently dehydrated to store. Store as you would any dehydrated food, in a cool, dark, dry place.

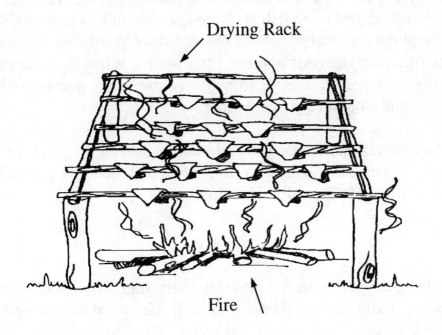

Drying Rack

Fire

Meat Recipes

Liver Pudding

If you don't like the taste of liver - here is a way for you to enjoy it and receive the high nutritional benefits of this wonderful organ meat. Grind liver and place in a pot. Season lightly with salt, pepper, herbs and spices to taste. Add sufficient water and fat and cook for approximately 4 hours on a slow boil, stirring occasionally. Transfer mixture to a crock of suitable size, filling from one half to three quarters full. Place crock in the oven and cook at 200ºF for about 4 more hours until the lard rises to the top. Melt an additional 2 cups of lard, add to the crock and cook another 1 to 2 hours. When the mixture has cooled, place it in a root cellar or cool dry place for storage. To use, clean lard off of top, heat and serve. This mixture should store nicely over winter.

To enhance the flavor of this recipe you can add other meats or organs in a ratio of 2/3 liver to other meats. Using the tongue or heart from a freshly butchered animal is a real treat and will enhance the nutritional value of this recipe.

Jerky

Cut beef, lamb, turkey, chicken or pork into very thin strips about 1/4 inch thick. Strip off any excess fat. Extra fat will shorten the shelf life, as fat can become rancid over time. Make a marinade of soy sauce, ginger and honey. One cup soy sauce, 1/4 cup honey and 1 tsp. of ginger. Expand the recipe proportionally depending upon how much meat you have to prepare. Soak the meat in the marinade for several days in the refrigerator. Keep checking marinade periodically to make sure that all strips are being evenly soaked. After sufficient soaking take strips out and place on an oven rack or your dehydrator. Slowly dehydrate in the oven for 24 hours at 125ºF. You do not want to cook the meat, you want to dehydrate it.

Sausage

Sausage is an excellent way to use pieces of meat that are too small for anything else. If you have any fat that you have not turned into tallow candles you may also add this. A general rule is one-third fat and two thirds lean meat. Be sure that all body areas and clots are cut away from the meat before using, as these will cause the meat to spoil. You will get a longer shelf life from your sausage if you cure it first.

Get a good meat grinder that has different sizes of grinding plates, 1/8 inch to 1/2 being most frequently used. Chilled meat grinds up better than warm meat. Grind the meat and add your herbs and other seasonings, mixing well. Regrind the meat after you have chilled it over night. This will disperse the herbs thoroughly through the meat.

Sausage may be stored in sterilized crocks and covered with melted lard until ready for use. It can be canned or smoked. Casings from the intestines of sheep, cattle and hogs are used to hold the sausage. Muslin sleeves can also be used for casings. Be sure that casings are tightly filled, with no air holes, as air will invite molds and spoilage. An attachment can be secured to go onto a sausage mill to attach the castings and muslin sleeves.   Here is a sample recipe:

4 pounds trimmings   5 tsp. salt
4 tsp. ground sage   4 tsp. ground pepper
1/2 tsp. ground cloves   1 tsp. ground nutmeg
1 tsp. salt

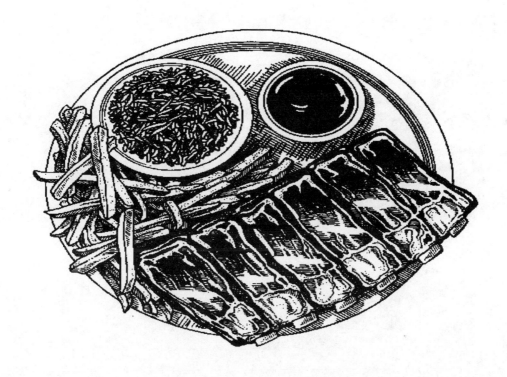

Recipes

Recipes

All of the following recipes can also use honey as a substitution for sugar. See honey substitution chart on page 183.

Whole Wheat Hot Pancakes

1 C. wheat flour
1 level t. baking powder
2 T. oil
2 T. Honey

1/4 t. salt
3/4 C. milk
1 large egg, beaten lightly

Sift dry ingredients. Combine milk and oil and add to dry ingredients. Then stir until moist but not too much. A cast iron skillet at medium heat is ideal. Use what you have.

Syrup: 1 C. water, honey, heat to boiling and add some maple flavoring, about 2 t. approx.

Fruit Syrup For Pancakes
(Fresh or dried)

Bring to boil, stirring constantly:
1/2 C. sugar
3 T. cornstarch
2 C. water (use fruit juice for part of water)
Add:
2 C. sliced peaches or other fruit. Simmer until fruit is tender. Add 2 T. lemon juice. Serve hot with pancake

Graham Crackers

1/2 C. evaporated milk
2 T. lemon juice or vinegar
1/2 C. honey
2 t. vanilla
1 t. salt
6 C. whole wheat flour (approx.)

1/2 C. water
1 C. packed brown sugar
1 C. vegetable oil
2 eggs, beaten lightly
1 t. soda

Mix together milk, water and lemon juice. In separate bowl beat well, sugar, honey, oil, vanilla and eggs. Combine mixtures with dry ingredients. Divide in 4 equal parts. Place each on a greased and floured cookie sheet and roll to about 1/8" thick. Prick with fork. Bake at 375° for about 15 minutes or until light brown. Remove from oven and cut in squares immediately.

Emergency Survival Bar

3 C. cereal (oatmeal, cornmeal, or wheat flakes)
2 1/2 C. powdered milk
1 C. sugar
3 T. honey
3 T. water
1/2 C. jello (optional)
1/4 t. salt

Place all dry ingredients except jello in a bowl. Bring water, honey, and jello to a boil. Add to dry ingredients. Mix. well. Add water a little at a time until mixture is just moist enough to mold. Place in a small square dish and dry in the oven under very low heat. Wrap and store. This will make 2 bars, each containing approx. 1,000 calories or enough food for one day. These will store for a long time and excellent for emergency packs, etc. Eat dry or cooked in about 3/4 C. water

Yummy Food Bar

1 C. finely ground figs
1 C. finely ground dates
3 C. water
1 heaping tablespoon yellow (unsifted) corn meal

Bring three cups water to boil, add figs and dates. cover and shut heat to minimum for approximately five minutes. Add corn meal while stirring and cook for additional 10 minutes. Serve with cream or as is.

Mayonnaise

1 whole egg
2 t. sugar
1/4 t. salt

1 1/2 T. vinegar
dash of pepper
1 C. oil

Put all ingredients in the blender, except for 3/4 C. of the oil. Blend together well. While blending slowly add the remaining oil until the mayonnaise is thick

Soy Milk

Soy milk is a good substitute for any one that is allergic to cow's milk. Soak 2 cups of soy beans for 12 hours. Change the water frequently. Grind soaked, raw beans with a fine blade on a food grinder. Add 6 cups water to the beans in a large pan. Cook until foamy for 1 hour. Put through a blender, then strain through a cheese cloth. Refrigerate.

Homemade Playdough

1 C. flour   1/2 C. salt
2 t. cream of tartar   1 t. oil
1 C. water   food coloring

Directions - Mix all ingredients together in a bowl into a dough-like consistency. Roll out on a bread board and cut into desired shapes or use as with clay and model.

♦ The foregoing recipes were all obtained from the book Cookin' With Home Storage written by Vicki Tate.

Recipes

Bean and Wheat Casserole

5 oz. bulgur wheat
14 oz. canned tomatoes
12 oz. mixed beans
1 onion
1 green pepper
3 carrots
1 lg. clove garlic
3 sticks celery

3 tablespoons oil
1 bayleaf
1 tablespoon tomato puree
1/2 teaspoon chili powder
sea salt
black pepper
breadcrumbs

Soak beans overnight, drain and rinse. Cover with cold water and cook gently until tender, approx. 1 hour. Peel and chop onion, pepper and crush garlic. Slice carrots and celery. Fry them all gently in oil with bayleaf for approx. 15 minutes. Remove bayleaf. Add bulgur wheat, tomatoes, puree and seasonings to vegetable mixture, along with drained beans.   Spoon mixture into a shallow greased casserole dish and sprinkle with breadcrumbs Dot with butter and bake for 30 minutes. Set oven for 375°.

Soy Loaf

6 oz. soy beans
1 onion
2 cloves garlic, crushed
4 stick celery
2 tomatoes, chopped
4 oz. breadcrumbs
1 teaspoon dried thyme

1 egg
2 tablespoons tomato puree
4 tablespoons chopped parsley
2 oz. butter
sea salt
black pepper

Soak beans overnight, rinse and cook for approx. 4 hours. Drain beans and mash them. Fry onion, garlic and celery in butter for about 15 minutes. Add tomatoes and tomato puree and cook gently for 5 more minutes. Stir in soy beans, breadcrumbs, parsley, thyme and egg. Season with salt and pepper.

Grease a 1 lb. loaf tin with butter, coat with dried crumbs. Spoon soy mixture into the tin and smooth down the top. Cover with foil and bake in oven for 1 hour. Oven at 375°.

Black Eyed Bean Bake

12 oz. black eye beans
2 onions
3 cloves garlic
3 tablespoons vegetable oil
1/2 teaspoon thyme

3/4 pint water or vegetable stock
black pepper
1 teaspoon marjoram
sea salt

Topping - whole wheat breadcrumbs and 2 oz. grated cheese

Soak, drain and rinse beans. Fry onions and garlic in oil for 10 minutes until tender. Add beans, herbs and water. Simmer gently about 30 - 45 minutes. Puree the bean mixture or pass through vegetable mill. Season with salt and pepper. Spoon in shallow dish and sprinkle with breadcrumbs and grated cheese. Bake for 30 minutes. Oven at 350º.

Red Bean Salad

6 oz red kidney beans
1 clove garlic, mashed
1 onion, sliced
1 tablespoon red wine vinegar
3 tablespoons olive oil

1/2 teaspoon sugar
1 tablespoon tomato puree
1/4 teaspoon dry mustard
sea salt
black pepper

Soak, cook and drain beans. Add onion and garlic to beans. Mix vinegar, oil, mustard, sugar, tomato puree, salt and pepper. Pour over bean mixture, stir well. Serve cold.

Tomato Sauce

1 onion, chopped
1 clove garlic, crushed
3 tablespoons vegetable oil
14 oz. can tomatoes

2 tablespoons tomato puree
sea salt
black pepper

Fry onion and garlic in oil, about 10 minutes. Add tomatoes and tomato puree. Bring mixture to boil and simmer for about 10-15 minutes. This will reduce liquid. Season with salt and pepper.

White Sauce

1 oz butter   salt
1 oz. flour   pepper
3/4 pint milk or cream   nutmeg

Melt butter in saucepan. Stir in flour and cook for several minutes, but don't brown. Remove from heat and add milk. Whisk milk, butter and flour together until smooth. Return to heat and simmer for 15 minutes. Season with salt, pepper and nutmeg.

Cheese Sauce
Make basic white sauce and add 4 oz. of grated cheese. Whisk until smooth.

Fritters

4 oz. flour   1/4 pint milk
pinch salt   1 teaspoon oil
1 egg   1 12 oz. can sweet corn

Mix salt and flour in large bowl. Add egg and beat until blended. Add milk and oil and beat again until smooth. Drain sweet corn and add to batter. Put tablespoonfuls of mixture into hot fat and fry on both sides.

Quick Stew

2 onions   1/2 pint stock or water
2 oz. butter   1 can tomatoes
1 small cabbage   1 can potatoes
Can green beans   1 can carrots
1 heaped tsp. mixed herbs   Salt and pepper to taste
1 bay leaf   2 tablespoons chopped parsley
2 tablespoons flour   1 can nutmeat

Chop onions and cook in butter in large pan for 5 min. Add cabbage to onions. Add herbs, bay leaf and flour. Stir well then add water, tomatoes, drained potatoes and carrots. Cut nutmeat into cubes and add. Cook until all vegetables are cooked through. Season to taste and serve with chopped parsley.

One Pan Meal

1 oz. butter	4 carrots
4 potatoes	1 bay leaf
2 onions, chopped	salt and pepper
1 can tomatoes	1 can containing meat of nuts
4 sticks celery, chopped	4 oz. green beans

Melt butter and add vegetables. Cook with bay leaf gently for ten minutes. Add can of tomatoes, salt and pepper to taste and a little vegetable stock to make more gravy. Simmer until tender. Add nutmeat. Heat through and serve.

Fluffy Ground Rice

2 oz ground rice	1/2 teaspoon almond essence
1 pint milk	honey to taste
1 egg, separated	nutmeg to taste
1/2 teaspoon vanilla	jelly

Mix ground rice to a smooth paste with a little milk. Scald remainder of milk and pour over ground rice, stirring continuously. Cook gently for 5 minutes. Remove from stove and mix in the beaten egg yolk. Return to stove and cook for 2 minutes. Add vanilla and almond. Sweeten with honey. Fold in the lightly beaten egg white. Serve hot or cold. Sprinkle with nutmeg and top with currant jelly.

Lentil Soup

1 oz. butter	1 bay leaf
1 onion	1/2 pint milk
1 carrot	2 tsp. lemon juice
4 oz. lentils	salt and pepper
1 1/2 pints water	

Melt butter and sauté carrots and onions until lightly browned. Add lentils, water and one bay leaf and cook for 1 hour. Pass through sieve or blender, return to pan, add milk, lemon juice and seasoning to taste.

Clear Vegetable Broth

1 stick celery
1 large carrot
1 onion
1/2 oz.butter
1 bay leaf

2 pints stock or water
1 Teaspoon chervil
2 Tablespoon chopped parsley
salt and pepper

Chop vegetables finely and cut onion into rings. Toss vegetables in melted butter, add bay leaf, chervil and stock. Simmer for about 15 minutes until vegetables are tender. Add chopped parsley and season to taste.

Black Bean Soup

3 Tablespoons olive oil
1 stalk celery, sliced
3 cloves garlic
1 Teaspoon celery salt
1/4 - 1/2 cup lemon juice

1 onion, chopped
1 1/2 cup black beans
6 cups vegetable stock
2 tablespoons whole wheat flour

Soak, drain and rinse black beans. Heat olive oil and sauté the onion and celery. Add the black beans, garlic and vegetable stock. Bring mixture to boil. Cover and simmer for 3 hours. Add celery salt and sift flour into soup. Remove from heat. Transfer to blender and puree. When entire mixture pureed return to pot and cook until soup thickens, or about 20 minutes. Stir in lemon juice to taste. Garnish soup with lemon slices.

Celery Potato Chowder

1 - 2 Tablespoons olive oil
1 bunch celery, chopped
2 cups water
2 Tablespoons butter
1 - 2 Teaspoons chives

1 small onion, chopped
3 medium potatoes, diced
2 Tablespoons whole wheat flour
4 cups milk
Sea salt

Sautè onion in oil until tender. Add celery, potatoes and water. Salt to taste. Bring mixture to boil, then simmer for 30 minutes. Melt butter in saucepan and whisk in flour. Gradually add milk, stirring constantly over medium heat. Allow to thicken. Add milk-flour mixture to celery-potato mixture and simmer until smooth. Top with chives and serve warm.

Squash or Pumpkin Soup

1 med. buttercup or butternut squash   4 - 5 cups water
1/4 Teaspoon sea salt   1 small onion
Chopped parsley   Sesame oil

Wash squash and remove the skin and seeds. Cut squash into large chunks. Put squash in pot and add water and salt. Bring to boil. Cover, lower heat and simmer until squash is soft, about 40 minutes to an hour. Sauté onion in sesame oil. Puree squash and return to pot. Add onion and simmer for several minutes. Serve with garnish.

Earthy Miso Soup

2 cups raw chopped cabbage   1/2 cup raw chopped carrots
1 1/2 Tablespoons butter   3 Tablespoons flour
1 Tablespoon tamari sauce   2 1/2 cups water
1/8 cup miso   1/8 cup fresh parsley

Chop and steam the cabbage and carrots. In a separate pot, melt butter, add in flour to make a paste. Add tamari and miso and whisk in water, stirring constantly. As mixture, thickens, add cooked vegetables. When cooking process finished, add fresh chopped parsley as a garnish.

Lentil and Barley Stew

1/4 cup butter   1/3 cup chopped onion
1/3 cup chopped celery   2 1/2 cups tomatoes
2 cups water   1/2 cup dried lentils, washed
1/3 cup whole barley   1/2 Teaspoon sea salt
1/8 Teaspoon black pepper   1/8 Teaspoon rosemary
1/3 cup shredded carrots

In a large heavy saucepan, melt the butter and sauté the onion until tender. Add celery and cook five minutes longer. Add remaining ingredients except the carrots. Bring to a boil, cover and simmer gently 25 minutes, stirring occasionally. Add carrots and cook five minutes longer or until barley and lentils are tender.

Easy Tomato Soup

1 cup dried powdered tomato
1 cup nonfat dry milk powder
1 Teaspoon dried crushed parsley

6 - 8 cups water
1/8 Teaspoon pepper

Mix tomato powder, 3 cups water, milk powder and pepper in blender. Add remaining water and heat to serve. Sprinkle with parsley.

Great Grains Casserole

4 cups millet, rice or buckwheat cooked
1 cup carrots, grated
1 cup green peppers, chopped
1 cup celery chopped
1 Tablespoon Parsley
1/4 cup nutritional yeast, optional
1 cup grated cheese

1 cups mushrooms, sliced
1 cups onion, chopped
1 Tablespoon Soy Sauce
1 Tablespoon salt
Tomato slices

Sautè green peppers, onion and celery. Mix vegetables, except for tomatoes, and grain together in a large bowl. Oil a casserole dish and begin to layer mixture with tomato slices until mixture used up. Add grated cheese to top of casserole. Place under broiler until golden brown or bake in oven at 350°F.

Soy Burgers

3 cups mashed cooked soy beans
1/4 cup chopped onion
1 Tablespoon parsley
1/2 cup wheat germ
1/2 cup bran
1 Tablespoon soy sauce
1 Tablespoon oregano
1 Tablespoon garlic salt
2 eggs

Mix all ingredients together and form into patties.
Roll patties in bran and sauté until golden brown.

Under the Broiler Sandwiches

1 1/2 cup carrots, grated
3/4 cup green pepper, chopped
1/4 cup onion, chopped
1 cup pinto bean spread
2 cups alfalfa sprouts

3/4 cup white colby cheese, grated
2 pita bread, small
1/2 cup tomato sauce
Dash paprika
4 thin slices tofu (optional)

Place pita bread face up on cookie sheet or broiler pan. Spread on bean spread and add ingredients in following order: bean spread, tomatoe sauce, veggies, tofu, maybe more sauce, cheese, paprika and fresh sprouts. Broil until cheese melts and is golden brown. If you don't have broiler, bake in oven until golden brown.

Pinto Bean Spread

1 cup pinto beans, cooked
1/2 Teaspoon cumin
1/2 Teaspoon chili powder

1/4 Teaspoon sea salt
1/4 Teaspoon garlic, granulated

To receive 3 cups cooked beans, cook 1 cup dry pinto beans with 3 cups water. Cook approximately 1 1/2 hours. Mash beans and add remaining ingredients.

Crusty Cornbean Pie

Quick cornmeal crust

2 cups yellow cornmeal
2 Tablespoons nutritional yeast
1/2 - 3/4 cup hot stock

1/2 Teaspoon salt
3 Tablespoons oil

Mix all ingredients and pat into oiled pie dish.

Filling

1 onion, chopped
1 celery stalk, chopped
3 Tablespoons soy sauce

1 carrot chopped
3 cups kidney beans cooked
1 Teaspoons cumin

Turn cooked ingredients into cornmeal crust. Bake at 350°F for about 25 minutes. Remove from oven, sprinkle with grated cheese, and bake for 5 minutes more.

Chick Pea Dish

1 cup chick peas
1 Tablespoon soy sauce
1 carrot diced
1/8 Teaspoon sea salt
parsley sprig

1 inch Kombu seaweed
1 onion diced
2 shitake mushrooms
1 Teaspoon sesame oil

Soak chick peas overnight in 3 cups water. Drain and reserve soaking water. Add beans to heavy saucepan, place kombu on the bottom. Add soaking water and enough fresh water to equal 4 cups. Bring rapidly to a boil, then lower heat to a gentle simmer for 2 - 3 hours. Sauté onion, carrots and mushrooms. Add to beans in last half hour of cooking, along with salt and soy sauce. Serve with garnished parsley.

Corn Meal Dish

2 cups corn meal
1/2 Teaspoons sea salt
1/2 cup sunflower seeds

6 cups water
1 medium leek

Dry roast corn meal in medium hot skillet until fragrant smell, avoid burning. Heat water and salt, adding roasted corn meal. Stir constantly with wire whisk, maintaining gentle simmer for 30-40 minutes Clean and chop leek, adding to simmering corn meal in the last 15-20 minutes. Roast sunflower seeds and then add last 5 minutes of simmering.

Tofu Chili

5 cups cooked pinto beans
1/4 cup soy sauce
3 Tablespoons corn oil
1/2 cup water
2 large onions diced
1 Tablespoon salt
2 Tablespoons cumin

2 lbs. frozen, fresh or dried tofu
1 1/2 tablespoons tomato paste
1/2 Teaspoon garlic powder
1 medium green pepper diced
3 cloves garlic
1 1/2 Tablespoons chili powder

Cut tofu into bite size pieces and freeze overnight. Thaw out the next day (about 1 hour). Mix ingredients minus pepper and onions with thawed tofu. Heat up in a skillet. Sauté onions and peppers. Add to skillet with tofu mixture and simmer together. Add spices and garlic cloves. Cook 20 40 minutes.

Ratatouille

1 pound zucchini
1 onion, sliced
2-3 cloves garlic, pressed
1 green pepper, chopped
1/8 Teaspoon pepper
1 1/2 Teaspoons thyme

1 small eggplant
1/4 cup olive oil
2 tomatoes, peeled and chopped
1 Teaspoon salt
1 Teaspoon basil

Cut zucchini and eggplant into 1/2 inch cubes. Sauté with onion in olive oil until tender. Stir in garlic, tomatoes, green peppers, salt, pepper, basil and thyme. Cook, covered on medium heat for 15 minutes. Serve over brown rice or other grain.

Algerian Couscous

1 cup chick-peas
2-3 Tablespoons olive oil
1 pound carrots, sliced 1/2 inch
1 cup butter
2 pounds zucchini, sliced
1 pound peas

3 cups couscous
1 1/2 cups onions, sliced
1/2 pound raisins
1/2 Teaspoon powdered ginger
3 pounds tomatoes, sliced
Salt and pepper to taste

Soak chick-peas overnight. Cook for one hour or until tender. Let couscous stand in 3 cups of water. Sauté onions. Add carrots and 5 cups of water. Bring to a boil and reduce heat. Simmer for 15 minutes until vegetables tender. Steam couscous for 15 minutes in steamer. Add 1/4 cup butter and turn into couscous. Sprinkle raisins over couscous and steam for another 15 minutes. Add seasonings, zucchini, tomatoes, chick-peas and peas to onion/carrot mixture and stir well. Simmer for 15 minutes. Remove couscous from heat and stir in remainder of butter. Serve couscous on plate and top with vegetable mixture.

Sprouts Slaw

1 1/2 cups alfalfa sprouts
1/2 cup grated carrot
1/4 cup minced onion

3 cups shredded cabbage
Salad dressing of your choice

Place all ingredients in a large mixing bowl and mix well. Just before serving, add dressing and mix again.

Four Bean Salad

1/2 cup dry chick-peas
1/2 cup dry kidney beans
1-2 carrots, grated
1/2 green pepper, chopped
Grated cheese

1/2 cup dry black beans
1/2 pound string beans, cut to 1 inch
3 scallions sliced
1 large stalk of celery, diced

Soak chick-peas, black beans and kidney beans in water overnight. Drain. Cook beans in unsalted water, cover for about an hour or until tender. Drain and chill. Steam string beans for 5 minutes or until tender. Chill. In large bowl combine vegetables and beans. Pour over dressing and refrigerate for several hours. Serve with grated cheese on top.

Dressing

1/2 cup olive oil
1 Teaspoon onion powder
1 Teaspoon basil
1/2 Teaspoon parsley flakes

1/3 cup apple cider vinegar
1 clove garlic, crushed
1/2 Teaspoon Oregano
Salt to taste

Put all ingredients in a covered jar and shake vigorously. Pour over bean mixture and chill.

Tomato Juice Salad Dressing

1/2 cup tomato juice
1 Teaspoon onion flakes
1/2 Teaspoon garlic powder
1/4 Teaspoon salt
Oregano to taste

2 Tablespoons apple cider vinegar
1/2 Teaspoon dry mustard
1/8 Teaspoon white pepper
1/2 Teaspoon parsley flakes

Combine all ingredients in jar with tight fitting lid. Shake well. Refrigerate. Allow to marinate for 2 to 3 hours before serving.

Basic Salad Dressing

1 1/2 Tablespoons cider vinegar
1/4 Teaspoon dry mustard
1/2 Teaspoon grated onion
5 Tablespoons olive oil

1 Teaspoon lemon juice
3 Tablespoons tomato juice
1 Teaspoon tarragon
1 clove garlic, crushed.

Fruit and Ginger Relish

1 cup raisins
1/2 cup apricots
1/4 inch piece ginger root, peeled
1 1/2 or 3 cups water

1/2 cup dates
1 tsp. cinnamon
1 lemon or orange peel
salt

Place all fruit ingredients in a saucepan and bring to boil slowly. Simmer 30 to 40 minutes. Slice ginger thinly and add to fruit. Add cinnamon. Cool and refrigerate until used.

Apple Date Butter

2 cups pitted dates
2 1/2 cups dehydrated apples
2 cups water
Nutmeg
1/2 Teaspoon cloves

Grated lemon rind
1/4 Teaspoon allspice
1/4 Teaspoon

Rehydrate apples. Place all ingredients in saucepan, mix well and cook uncovered until apples are tender and mixture is thick, approx. 30 minutes. Puree or blend together. Refrigerate before serving.

Apricot Nut Bread

3/4 cup boiling water
1 cup dried apricots
1 Tablespoon baking powder
2 eggs
1 cup chopped nuts

1/3 cup butter
3 cups flour
1/2 Teaspoon salt
1/2 cup honey
1/2 cup light corn syrup

Grease loaf pan. Rehydrate apricots with boiling water. Mix flour, baking powder and salt. Blend butter, honey, eggs and corn syrup until smooth. Stir in apricots with water they were soaking in. Stir in nuts. Gradually add dry ingredients. Pour into loaf pan and bake at 350°F for 1 hour and 15 minutes.

Banana Bars

1/4 cup butter
1/2 cup honey
2 eggs
2 cups whole wheat flour
2 Teaspoons baking powder

1/2 Teaspoon salt
1 cup dried banana slices
1/2 Teaspoon lemon extract
1/2 Teaspoon vanilla

Reconstitute bananas by placing in boiling water and letting them soften. When soft, mash until smooth. Cream together butter and honey. Add eggs and beat well. Add bananas. Sift together flour, baking powder and salt. Add flour mixture to banana mixture. Add lemon and vanilla. Mix well. Spread into greased 9 x 13 pan. Bake at 350°F for 30 minutes.

Carrot Cake

3/4 cup butter
1/2 cup honey
1/4 Teaspoon baking soda
2 cups dehydrated carrots
2 eggs beaten
1/3 cup sour milk (1/3 cup milk plus 1 tsp. vinegar)

2 cup whole wheat flour
1 Tablespoon baking powder
1 Teaspoon salt
1/2 Teaspoon cinnamon
2/3 cup chopped pecans

Rehydrate carrots. Cream butter and honey. Add carrots and eggs to creamed mixture. Sift dry ingredients and add nuts. Add dry ingredients and milk alternately to creamed mixture. Pour into two greased 9 inch cake pans. Bake at 350°F for 35 minutes. Top with cream cheese frosting.

Cream Cheese Frosting

1/2 cup cream cheese
1 1/2 Teaspoons vanilla
1 cup honey

6 Tablespoons butter
1 Tablespoon milk

Cream cheese and butter. Add vanilla, milk and honey. Mix until smooth and of spreading consistency. Add to Carrot Cake.

Applesauce Cake

1 1/2 cup whole wheat flour
1/2 cup honey
1/2 Teaspoon vanilla
1 Teaspoon Baking Soda
1/2 Teaspoon salt

1/2 cup oil
1 Teaspoon vinegar
1/2 cup chopped almonds
1/2 cup applesauce
1/2 cup water

Cream oil and honey together. Add water, applesauce, vinegar and vanilla. Mix flour, soda, salt and almonds. Combine wet and dry ingredients and pour into a greased 8 x 8 x 2 inch pan. Bake at 350ºF for 35-40 minutes.

Date Cookies

1/2 cup butter
1/2 cup honey
1 egg
2 cups chopped dates
1/2 cup chopped pecans

2 cups whole wheat flour
1/2 Teaspoon cream tarter
1/2 Teaspoon baking soda
1/2 Teaspoon vanilla

Cream honey and butter. Add egg and vanilla. Mix dry ingredients together. Add to creamed mixture. Make into two rolls. Place in refrigerator or chill over night. Slice to about 1/2 inch thick and bake at 350ºF for 25 minutes.

Pastry Crust

1 1/2 cups whole wheat pastry flour
1/2 Teaspoon honey
3/4 Teaspoon salt
1/2 cup oil
2 Tablespoons milk

Combine flour and salt. Beat oil, honey and milk together. Mix flour and oil mixture with fork. Roll into crust and place in 9 inch pie pan. Flute edges.

Dried Fruit Bars

1 cup dried fruit
1/2 cup honey
1/2 teaspoon cinnamon
1 cup oatmeal
1/2 Teaspoon nutmeg
1/2 Teaspoon cloves

1/2 Teaspoon baking soda
1/2 cup oil
1 egg
1/2 Teaspoon salt
1 cup whole wheat flour

Rehydrate fruit in 1/3 cup boiling water. This can be any fruit, apples, apricots, bananas, etc. Add baking soda to fruit mixture. Cream oil and honey and add egg. Combine all dry ingredients and mix well. Spread evenly into well-greased 9 x 13 inch baking pan. Bake at 350°F for 20 minutes. Cool for 15 minutes before cutting.

Peach Muffins

2 cups whole wheat flour
2/3 cup dry milk
1/8 cup honey
1 Tablespoon baking powder
1 Teaspoon salt
1/2 Teaspoon cinnamon

1/4 teaspoon nutmeg
1 cup dried peaches
1 egg, beaten
1 cup water
1/4 cup oil

Rehydrate peaches. Combine flour, instant milk, baking powder, salt, cinnamon and nutmeg. Cream oil and honey. Add egg, water and peaches. Stir egg mixture into dry ingredients. Spoon into muffin tin or cups. Bake at 400°F for 20 - 25 minutes.

No Crust Peach Pie

1/4 cup honey
1 cup flour
1/2 Teaspoon nutmeg

1/2 square butter
1/2 Teaspoon salt

Rehydrate 3 cups of dried peaches. Place in 9-inch deep dish pie plate with crust on bottom. Cream honey and butter. Add dry ingredients. Sprinkle over top of peaches. Bake at 400°F for 30 minutes.

Whole Wheat Pretzels

1 tablespoon yeast
1 tablespoon honey
3 1/2 cup whole wheat bread flour
3 tablespoons oil
Optional toppings: course sea salt
  sesame seeds, poppy seeds

1 1/2 cup warm water
1 teaspoon sea salt
1/2 cup wheat germ
1 egg with 1 tablespoon water for glaze

Dissolve yeast water with honey. When bubbly, stir in salt and oil and 2 cups flour. Beat until smooth. Add wheat germ and remaining flour to make a soft dough. Knead until smooth and elastic, about 5 minutes. Let rise until doubled, 45-60 minutes. Punch down and divide into 16 equal parts. Roll each piece into a rope 16 inches long. Transfer pretzels to greased baking sheets and let rise 20 minutes. Bake at 400°F for about 20 minutes or until golden brown.

Carob & Honey Brownies

1/2 cup butter
2/3 cup honey
2 eggs
1 teaspoon vanilla
1/2 teaspoon salt

1/2 cup carob powder
2/3 cup whole wheat pastry flour
1 teaspoon baking powder
1 cup chopped nuts
3 tablespoons milk

Cream honey and butter together. Beat in eggs, one at a time. Beat in vanilla and salt. Sift together carob, flour and baking powder. Stir dry mixture with nuts and milk into a batter. Turn into an oiled 9 inch square pan. Bake at 350°F for 30 minutes.

Dandy Candy

1 cup peanut butter
2 teaspoon vanilla
1 cup tahini
2 cups granola mix
1/2 cup maple syrup

1 cup dry buttermilk
1 cup raisins
1/2 cup honey
1 cup instant dry milk
1/4 cup sesame seeds

Mix peanut butter, honey and maple syrup together. Add raisins, tahini, sesame seeds and granola mix. Add buttermilk and vanilla. Mix well and press into 9 x 14 inch pan. No need to bake.

Bread Pudding

Enough bread crumbs to fill baking dish
3 eggs   1 pint milk
3 tablespoons honey   Nutmeg

Spread bread with butter, enough to fill baking dish. Mix eggs, honey and milk together. Pour over bread and sprinkle with nutmeg. Bake at 350°F for 20 to 30 minutes. You can add your favorite fruit to this, such as pears, peaches, apples, etc.

Peanut Butter Rolls

2 cups peanut butter   1 cup honey
1 cup granola or oatmeal

Mix together all ingredients and form into balls. Roll in coconut, sesame seed, etc. Chill.

Honey Popcorn Nut Crunch

1/2 cup melted butter   1/2 cup honey
3 quarts popcorn (popped)   1 cup chopped nuts

Preheat oven to 350°F. Blend honey and butter together and heat gently. Mix popcorn with nuts. Pour butter and honey mixture over popcorn. Mix well. Spread on cookie sheet thinly. Bake 10 - 15 minutes or until crisp.

Oatmeal Cookies

1 cup corn or canola oil or butter   1/2 cup honey
2 eggs   1 3/4 cup pastry flour
1 Teaspoon baking soda   1 Teaspoon baking powder
1/2 Teaspoon salt   1 Teaspoon cinnamon
1/2 Teaspoon nutmeg   1 cup raisins
3 cup oats   1/2 cup chopped or ground walnuts

Cream butter and honey. Add eggs. Mix with all dry ingredients. Spoon onto greased cookie sheets. Bake at 350° for 10-15 minutes.

Poppyseed Cake

1/2 cup Poppyseed
1/2 cup milk
1 stick butter - softened
1/2 cup honey
2 eggs

1 1/2 teaspoons baking powder
1/4 teaspoons salt
1/4 teaspoons vanilla
1/2 teaspoon lemon rind
1 cup whole wheat flour

Preheat oven to 350°F. Heat Poppyseed and milk together in a saucepan until it boils. Remove from heat and set aside. Cream butter and honey. Add eggs 1 at a time, beating well. Now combine all ingredients and again beat well. Bake in a well-greased loaf pan 40-50 minutes.

Spice Layer Cake

3/4 cup melted butter
2 1/4 cups whole wheat flour
1 teaspoon salt
3/4 teaspoon cinnamon
3/4 teaspoon cloves
3/4 cup water

3/4 cup honey
1 teaspoon baking powder
3/4 teaspoon soda
3 tablespoons buttermilk powder
3 eggs

Preheat oven to 350°. Cream butter and honey. Sift in flour, baking powder, salt, soda and spices. Add buttermilk. Mix until all flour is dampened; beat vigorously. Add eggs; beat 2 minutes more. Bake in 2 nine inch diameter round pans for 30 - 35 minutes.

Buttercream Frosting

1/2 cup honey
1 Teaspoon vanilla

2 Tablespoons butter
1/2 to 1 cup dry milk powder

Cream butter and honey. Add vanilla. Add milk slowly and beat until smooth. Let icing sit for awhile before spreading or chill in refrigerator.

Yummy Custard

4 large eggs
2 cups milk or soy milk
1/4 cup melted butter
1 cup dried fruit
  apples, peaches, apricots, etc.

1/2 cup honey
1/2 cup whole wheat pastry flour
1 Teaspoon vanilla

In a medium bowl, whisk together in order, eggs, honey, milk, flour, melted butter and vanilla. Stir in the dried fruit. Pour the mixture into a buttered 9 inch glass pie dish and bake 35-40 minutes at 350°F or until knife inserted 2 inches comes out clean. Cool or chill before serving. We tried this several ways, with dried apples and rhubarb. You can also vary the recipe by adding 1/2 teaspoon each of baking powder and baking soda.

Household Products

Basic Household Products

For a complete survival program there are certain household necessities that should be kept on hand and stored for future use. These are items that you will be using to clean, disinfect and generally maintain a household. The list below indicates useful items for general house cleaning and personal care maintenance.

Household Items		Personal Care Items
Hand soap	Lamps	Shampoo
Borax	Cheap light	Toothpaste
Clorox	Scissors	Vaseline
Liquid detergent	Hand clippers	Hair Conditioner
All-purpose cleaner	Steel wool	Lotion
Laundry detergent	String	Brushes
Disinfectant	Cord or Rope	Combs
Toothbrushes	Household oil	Deodorant
Baking soda	Insect Repellent	Nail Clippers
Toilet paper	Matches - Waterless	Small Hand Tools
Razor Blades	Sheets	
Paraffin wax	Washcloths	
Cheesecloth	Towels	
Aluminum foil	Blankets	
Waterproofing for cloth & leather	Candles - 7 day	
Writing paper supplies	Canning Jars	
Brooms	Sewing supplies	
Scrub Brushes	Bolts of cloth	
Mops	Thread	
Vinegar	Needles	
Stainless steel waterless	Yarn	
cookware	Zippers	
Lantern	Buttons	
	Reusable - canning jar lids	

Many of the above listed items can be made from simple materials. If you are unable to store a sufficient quantity of some of these household and personal care products, you should consider gathering raw materials together and making these items later when you need them.

Soap

The three main ingredients for making soap are water, fat and lye. All soaps have various proportions of these three ingredients. You can add your own scents and coloring agents according to your preference. Scent can be added by putting in some aromatic oils and coloring can be added by putting in some simple vegetable food coloring dyes. What makes the difference in soaps is the kind of fat used, the kind of lye, and how much of each. Lye made from wood ash produces soft soap. Soap made from commercial lye (sodium hydroxide) will be hard. Soaps containing coconut oil tend to lather well in cold water, but may be drying to the skin. Superfatted soaps, such as castile, are particularly gentle.

Lye preparation: Obtain a large wooden container. Place a hole near the bottom of the container on the side. This will allow the water to seep through the ashes and into another container below. Collect ashes from any burned hardwood, preferably oak, hickory, sugar maple, beech or any fruit wood. Place the ashes in the barrel. Scoop out a depression at the top of the ashes large enough to hold 2 to 3 quarts of water. Fill the depression with rainwater heated to boiling. Let the water seep down through the ashes. Continue to add water. It might be a while before the lye begins to trickle out the bottom. Do not attempt to hurry the process by stirring the ashes. What comes out the hole near the bottom of the container is the lye solution. This solution can be crystallized for convenience to a potash solution by boiling down in a stainless steel or enamelware pot. Maintain heat and eventually a grayish-white potash will be left remaining. Be aware that lye is highly caustic and should be washed immediately if it comes in contact with skin.

Fat preparation: Any animal fat and most vegetable oils can be used to make soap. The most satisfactory soap is made from a combination of beef fat (tallow) and pig fat (lard). Poultry fat needs to be combined with other fats, as alone it is too soft. First you need to render (extract by melting) the fat, which will purify the fat solids. Start with twice the weight of fat called for in the recipe. Cut fat into small pieces and heat over a low flame. Do not let fat burn or smoke. Strain this liquid fat into a clean container through cheesecloth and refrigerate until it is needed. If you want to deodorize the fat, cook sliced-up potatoes in the clarified fat. Use one potato for each 3 pounds of fat.

Making Soap

Materials to have on hand:
> 2 quart juice bottle to hold lye solution. Punch two holes in cover so you will
> > be able to pour lye over fat.

A 10 - 12 quart pot to hold the fat and lye.

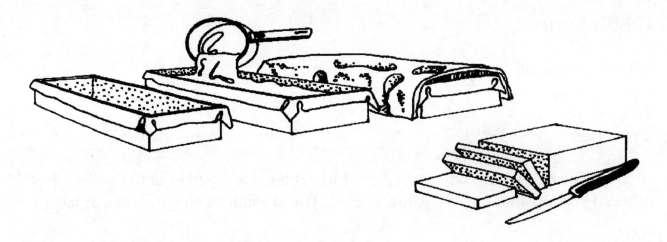

A wooden spoon to stir the lye solution and fat.

A candy or dairy thermometer that is accurate to within 1°F in the 80 - 120°F range.

Rubber gloves.

Molds for the soap.

Insulation to keep the soap warm after it is poured into the molds.

Newspapers to cover working surfaces.

Begin soap making process with a cool lye solution and warm fat already prepared. Depending upon the recipe you are using, bring the fat and lye solutions independently to a temperature of 95 - 98°. This can be done by placing their containers in basins of hot water and warming the water until the desired temperature is reached. Combine these two ingredients in another container and thoroughly stir them until mixed well. The mixture will turn opaque and brownish, then lighten. The soap is ready when its surface can support a drop of mixture for a moment, with a consistency of sour cream. This takes anywhere from 5 - 15 minutes. Add any colorants or scents at this stage. Pour this liquid into your mold and let dry slowly. Add some form of insulation to cover the mold for slow curing. Remove soap from molds after 24 hours.

Soap Recipes

Hand Soap

1 tablespoon lye
1/2 cup lukewarm fat
1/4 cup cold water
1 tablespoon lemon juice

Stir lye into water and dissolve. Combine fat together until they thicken. Add lemon juice and mix thoroughly. Pour into molds and air dry for two weeks.

Castile Soap

1 lb. 9 oz. olive oil
3 lb. 10 oz. tallow
10.5 oz. lye
2 pt. water

Mix crystallized lye and water together. Mix fat and lye together until thickened. Add olive oil and mix thoroughly. Allow to cool. (Read cautions on lye container label.)

Laundry Soap

2.5 qts. rain water preferred or regular water
2 qts. fat
1 cup clorox
1 small can lye, approximately 4 oz.
3 tablespoon borax

Mix water, clorox, borax and lye together. Add fat slowly. Remove from heat and leave in pot for two days to cure. Pour into other container for later use.

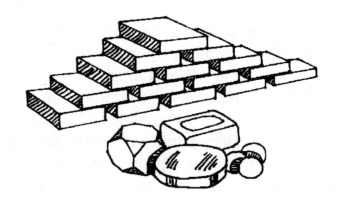

Shampoo

1 bar of basic soap
4 qts. water
2 slightly beaten whole eggs
1 teaspoon borax

Dissolve soap in boiling water. Let cool. Add eggs and borax. Mix thoroughly. Cool and pour into container for later use.

Toothpaste

Toothpaste #1.   Mix together ground charcoal and honey.
Toothpaste #2.   Create a paste of salt, water and bicarbonate of soda.

Deodorant

1.   Diluted cider vinegar, apply to body.

2.   A few drops of lavender oil applied to body.

3.   Infusion (boiled down to essence) of sage applied to body.

Lemon is an excellent ingredient to add to any cleanser or can be used alone diluted with warm water to clean any surface, whether it be your house or your body. Store diluted lemon extract.

Cider vinegar can be diluted and used as a window cleaner. Store both white and cider vinegar.

Basic Soap Chart

The following chart gives guidelines for making bulk soap batches

FATS	LYE	WATER
1 cup	2 Tbsp.	1/2 cup
2 cups	1/4 cup	3/4 cup
3 cups	1/4 cup + 2 Tbsp.	1 cup
4 cups	1/2 cup	1 1/2 cups
5 cups	1/2 cup + 2 Tbsp.	2 cups
6 cups	3/4 cup	2 1/4 cups
7 cups	3/4 cup + 2 Tbsp.	2 3/4 cups
8 cups	1 cup	3 cups
9 cups	1 cup + 2 Tbsp.	3 1/2 cups
10 cups	1 1/4 cups	3 3/4 cups
11 cups	1 1/4 cups + 2 Tbsp.	4 cups
12 cups	1 1/2 cups	4 1/2 cups

The following proportions should be remembered when adding or changing ingredients:

Fine vegetable oils:	**20% of total fats**
Essential oils:	**1 - 2% of total volume**
Antiseptic oils:	**2 - 10% of total volume**
Fillers: *	**10 - 20% of total volume**

*Fillers - These are additives to the soap that change the texture and quality of soap. Some favorite fillers are pumice used for heavy-duty cleaning, as well as bran, cornmeal, maize and oatmeal. Paraffin and beeswax are used to extend the soap and make it softer to the touch. Silica gives soap a silky texture. Grains and vegetable additives can be added but must be used with wheat germ oil or vitamin E oil to extend the shelf life.

Household Tips

There are many tried and true household hints that mothers pass on to daughters and friends to friends. Usually the only way you ever hear about these is word of mouth. We thought we would print what we felt was useful and interesting. Some of these tips could be helpful when you least expect it.

Kitchen

- **Pancake Syrup** - To make an inexpensive syrup for pancakes, save small amounts of leftover jams and jellies in one container. Fruit-flavored syrup can be made by adding 1 cup of honey to one cup of any kind of fruit juice and cooking it until it boils.

- **Jelly Jars** - Before discarding jam and jelly jars, fill with hot water and shake. Use the water when making gelatin desserts.

- **Stopping Boil Overs** - Spaghetti will not boil over or stick together if you add a small piece of butter or a few teaspoons of oil to the water. The same holds for rice.

- **Sticky Liquids** - To measure honey or other sticky syrups, oil the measuring cup with cooking oil and rinse under hot water first.

- **Cabbage Smell** - To avoid the awful odor of cooking cabbage or onions, add a lemon wedge to the pot.

- **Sugar Substitute** - Maple syrup may be substituted for sugar when making applesauce or apple pie, or many other recipes - Try it!

- **Onions Minus Tears** - Peel under cool water or refrigerate before chopping.

- **How to Chop Garlic** - Chop in a small amount of salt to prevent pieces from sticking to the knife or chopping board. Then pulverize with the tip of the knife.

- **Easily Peeled Tomatoes** - Place tomatoes in a bowl, add boiling water and let them stand for one minute. Tomatoes will peel easily with a sharp knife.

- **Cooking Dried Beans** - When cooking dried beans, add salt approximately 1/2 hour before they are to be done; if salt is added at the start, it will slow the cooking process.

- **Fresh Garlic** - Peel garlic and store in a covered jar of vegetable oil. The garlic will stay fresh and the oil will be nicely flavored for salad dressings.

- **Crackless Eggs** - Pierce the rounded end of eggs with a needle before hard-boiling to prevent shells from cracking.

- **Separated Eggs** - Use a small funnel to easily separate the egg white from the yolk. The yolk will remain in funnel while the white will fall through.

- **Nutritious Rice** - Cook rice in liquid saved from cooking vegetables to add flavor and nutrition. A nutty taste can be achieved by adding wheat germ to the rice.

Tips on Eggs

- **Fresh or Stale** - To find out if an egg is fresh, immerse in a pan of salted water. If egg rises it is stale, if it sinks it is fresh.

- **Fresh or Hard Boiled** - Spin the egg. If it wobbles it is raw - if it spins easily, it's hard boiled.

- **Poached Eggs** - Add a few drops of vinegar to the water when poaching an egg to keep it from running all over the pan.

- **Cracked Shell** - A couple of drops of vinegar will keep cracked eggs from running out of the shell when boiling.

- **Removing Eggshells** - Quickly rinse hot hard-boiled eggs in cold water, and the shells will be easier to remove.

Tips on Temperatures

- **Keeping It Hot** - A roast will stay hot for an hour or longer if you double-wrap it in foil or ten or more thicknesses of newspaper. Reflectex (insulating material) works great also.

- **Maintaining Heat** - By putting hot foods in insulated cooler, they'll stay hot if they are covered or wrapped.

Clean Up Tips

- **Burnt Food In Pan** - Boil water in the pan to loosen food. Or sprinkle baking soda generously over the burned food and moisten with water. Let stand for a few hours.

- **Clogged Drain** - To a grease-clogged drain, pour a cup each of salt and baking soda followed by a boiling kettle of water. This will generally open the drain.

- **Refrigerator Odor** - A cotton ball soaked with vanilla or an opened box of baking soda set on the lower shelf of the refrigerator will eliminate odor.

Keeping Food Fresh

- **Onions** - Wrap individually in foil or zip lock bag to keep them from becoming soft or sprouting.

- **Cheese** - Wrap cheese in a vinegar-dampened cloth or zip lock bag to keep it from drying out.

- **Lemons** - Lemons will be juicier if stored in a sealed jar of water in the refrigerator.

- **Smoked Meats** - Wrap ham or bacon in a vinegar-soaked cloth, then in waxed paper to preserve freshness.

- **Vegetables with Tops** - Remove the tops on carrots, beets, etc. before storing.

- **Potatoes** - Store an apple or two in with your freshly dug potatoes to preserve them. Seal in poly-bucket and add old newspapers to absorb moisture.

Personal Grooming

- **Vinegar for Skin** - The natural ph-balance will be restored to your skin by adding 2 teaspoons of apple cider vinegar to a bowl of warm water and splashing it on your face. Allow to air-dry.

- **Health Spa Secret** - After washing your face, rub a small amount of petroleum jelly into wet skin. Keep wetting face until the jelly does not feel greasy.

- **Cuticle Treatment** - Apply a mixture of equal parts of castor oil and white iodine to your cuticles every night.

- **Surgeon's Secret** - Apply odorless castor oil around eyes nightly. Plastic surgeons use this on their patients after surgery.

- **Insect Bite Remedies** - Try one of the following for relief of insect bites: apple cider vinegar applied to the affected area; a paste of baking soda and water allowed to dry on bites; or a past of meat tenderizer and water applied to bites.

- **Skin Treatment** - A wonderful relief for sunburn pain is the application of mint-flavored milk of magnesia to the skin. Good for applying to oily skin before bed.

- **Homemade Deodorant** - Heat in a double boiler until a smooth cream forms: equal parts of baking soda, petroleum jelly and talcum powder. This homemade deodorant can be kept in small jars and used like a regular cream deodorant.

- **Baking Soda Uses** - For a mouthwash: 1 teaspoon dissolved in 1/2 glass of water; for toothpaste, use full strength on your toothbrush; for burns, apply a paste of baking soda and water; for cleaning rough knees and elbows, a paste of soda and water.

- **Soft Hands** - Rinse hands in vinegar water after hand-washing clothes or dishes.

- **Tired Eyes** - Fresh cucumber slices applied to closed eyelids will freshen and revive tired eyes.

- **Sticky Bandages** - Peanut butter will remove tar and bandage residue from small children.

- **Removing Mildew From Books** - Dust book pages with cornstarch and let it stand for a few days before brushing off - this may remove mildew.

SEWING TIPS

- **Sharp Machine Needles** - Sharpen sewing machine needles by stitching through fine sandpaper.

- **Heavy Seams** - Rub seams with a bar of soap to allow a sewing machine needle to easily pass through.

- **Button Storage** - Buttons can be stored in empty pill bottles with snap-on tops.

- **Needle Holder** - An empty thermometer case is ideal for holding long and fine needles that may easily be lost in a sewing kit.

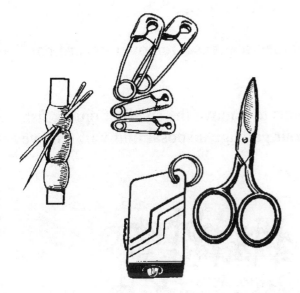

- **Long-Lasting Buttons** - Coat the center of buttons with clear nail polish and they'll stay on longer.

- **Another Button Tip** - On a four-hole button, sew through two holes at a time, knotting the thread and tying off for each set of holes. If one set should break, the other will still hold.

- **Sewing Accessories** - Rummage sales and thrift shops are good sources for finding unusual buttons and trims.

- **Emergency Thimble** - When hand-sewing and unable to find a thimble, wrap a couple of Band-Aids across the end of your finger.

- **Spool Storage** - Use an egg carton to store spools of thread.

- **Sewing Tip** - Instead of groping around your floor for fallen needles and pins, keep a magnet in your sewing kit. Simply sweep it across your rug to pick up those strays.

- **Stuck Zippers** - If a zipper sticks, run a bar of soap over it and it will slide easily.

- **Mending Gloves** - An old-fashioned clothespin can be inserted into the finger of a glove that needs repairing.

- **Eyeglasses Case** - An attractive case of glasses can be made by folding a pretty pot holder in half and stitching across the bottom and up one side.

- **Blue Jean Blanket** - Save good portions of worn-out blue jeans and stitch irregular patches together to make a sturdy beach blanket.

Stain and Spot Removal Hints

- **Blood Stains** - Apply meat tenderizer to stained area. Add warm water to make a paste. Wait 15 to 30 minutes and sponge with cool water. Pre-soaking may be necessary before laundering.

- **Mildew Stains** - Soak in a solution of 1 teaspoon of bleach per quart of water, or sponge with vinegar.

- **Grease Remover** - An effective and non-abrasive grease remover is ordinary shampoo.

- **Odor Remover** - Apply lemon juice to your hands to remove the smell of onion, fish or other strong odors. A lemon ground up in your garbage disposal unit will remove any odors in it, and give your kitchen a fresh smell.

- **Fresh Smelling Closet** - Put cloves, pine needles or mothballs in an old stocking and hang in your closet.

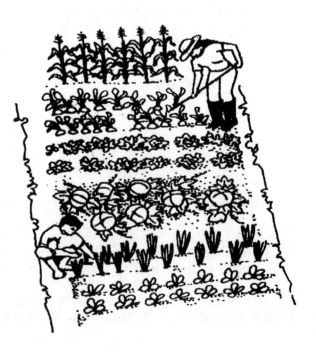

Gardening Hints

- **Natural Insecticide** - Add onions and garlic to a jar of water, let it stand for a week, and spray plants with it.

- **Removing Poison Ivy** - Mix a gallon of soapy water and 3 pounds of salt and spray the area.

- **Grow Parsley** - Wet a clean sponge and sprinkle with parsley. Place near a window and you will soon have a large clump of foliage.

- **Rabbit Plague** - Dust the cheapest talcum powder you can find around the base of your vegetable plants outside and it will quickly rid you of rabbit and flea beetle pests.

- **Sowing Seeds** - Use a salt shaker to sow seeds in your garden - it will distribute the seeds more evenly.

- **Watering Seedlings** - Push a drinking straw into the soil and funnel water into it to avoid disturbing new seedlings.

- **Killing Weeds** - Pour boiling water on grass or weeds growing between sections of sidewalk.

- **Window Boxes** - To keep rain from splattering dirt on your windows, put a layer of gravel on top of your windowboxes.

- **Egg Water** - Use the water in which eggs have been boiled to water plants - a good source of minerals.

- **Deer Control** - Save urine and pour all the way around garden - human scent repells them.

- **Germinating New Seeds** - Put seeds on the South pole of a magnet for 6 - 8 hrs. Will accelerate productivity and disease resistance.

Miscellaneous

- **Storing Clothing** - Keep out of season clothing moisture proof by storing in lidded plastic garbage cans.

- **Storing Paint** - Store paint containers upside down with the lids tightly fitted to prevent skin from forming on the surface.

- **Paintbrushes** - Soak brushes containing hardened paint in hot vinegar. Then wash in warm, sudsy water. Use for enamel or latex.

- **Paintbrushes** - When using latex paint, wrap brush tightly in plastic and put in freezer until next use.

- **Corroded Battery** - A strong solution of baking soda and water can be used to scrub battery terminal to prevent corrosion, or spread petroleum jelly on terminals.

- **Emergency Sewing Kit** - Take an empty book of matches and insert several needles in the space where the matches were torn out. Close the cover and wind several different colors of thread around it. It will come in handy sooner or later - just tuck in a pocket or purse.

- **Stubborn Knots** - Try dusting talcum powder on a very difficult knot.

- **Time Saver** - When making a move to a new town, be sure and take along a telephone book from your old town. It will be referred to for months for addresses, references, etc.

- **Candle Drippings** - For spilled wax on carpet, use a brown paper bag as a blotter and run a hot iron over it, which will absorb the wax.

- **Storage Idea** - When storing many boxes in the basement or attic, number each box. Tape a list to the wall containing an itemized account of the contents of each box next to the corresponding number.

- **Saving Water** - To conserve water when taking a shower, wet yourself down and turn the water off. After soaping, turn the water back on and rinse off. This will conserve as much as five gallons of water.

- **Emergency Raincoat** - A plastic garbage can liner makes a great emergency raincoat.

- **Increase Life of Sandals** - Lengthen the wearing life of sandals by putting adhesive tape on the inside of sandal straps.

- **General Rule to Remember** - To unscrew most anything, left is loose and right is tight. (Lefty-loosey - Righty-tighty) [Except propane or a few other strange fittings]

- **Corrosion Preventative** - Put a piece of charcoal in your toolbox to prevent corroded tools.

- **Safety Tip** - To keep the shut-off valves on water pipes from sticking, turn them every six months or so.

- **Sweater Dryer** - Use an old window screen (with fiberglass screening) to dry sweaters.

- **Dry Mittens** - Wet mittens can be dried quickly by pulling them over the bottom of a small jar and setting the open end of the jar atop a radiator.

- **Slip-Proof Wallet** - Fasten a large rubber band around your wallet to keep it from slipping out of your pocket.

- **Clothing Storage** - Put cloves in the pockets of winter coats or sweater bags to keep moths away.

- **Removing Burrs** - Crush burrs with a pair of pliers and brush out of dog's coat.

- **Fireplace Tip** - Soot can be reduced by two-thirds by occasionally throwing salt on the logs.

- **Clean Candles** - Clean candles with a cotton ball dipped in rubbing alcohol.

- **Candlesticks That Fit** - Soften the base of candles in hot water. When pliable, insert into holder.

- **If You Have Candles That Drip Too Fast** - Before burning candles, put them in the freezer for a few hours. They'll burn more slowly and evenly.

- **Disposable Apron** - An inexpensive apron for messy chores can be made easily and then discarded by slipping on a large plastic garbage-can liner. Cut neck and arm holes in it. Excellent emergency raincoat.

- **Non-sliding Dishes** - Crumple a paper towel and insert under a bowl or board to keep it from sliding when mixing ingredients or kneading and rolling dough.

- **Removing Ticks From Dogs** - Saturate a cotton swab with cleaning fluid and touch it to the head of the tick. Use a tweezer to pluck the tick out.

Ways to Use Empty Poly Buckets

Poly buckets are the 6 gallon food buckets that most nitrogen packed grains and legumes come packed in. You can also purchase empty poly buckets. If you have buckets that are left after you have emptied or eaten some of your stored food there are numerous ways to reuse these buckets. Instead of discarding or assuming that these buckets are only good for storing food, look through the following list of ideas. This will help you get maximum use of your buckets. If you come up with other ideas, let us know.

Garden Uses
- To do your worm composting in.
- Planters for tomatoes, peppers, egg plants, cucumbers or squash, etc.
- To carry compost and chicken manure to raised beds.
- For picking fruit off of your trees.
- As a micro composter. Create one each week. Fill your bucket only half full. Pound the lid on securely and roll around to aerate from time to time. Works very fast-only two to three weeks.
- To make "manure tea" fertilizer. Fill a burlap bag full of manure. Tie off the top securely. Attach a rope to the bag and dunk it or soak it in water till the water is appropriately brown.
- To store your root crops in between layers of damp sand. Seal tightly. Keep as cool as possible without freezing.

Uses Around the House
- To store laundry soap in.
- Catching rainwater - inside or out.
- As a laundry basket.
- To put under sink to separate aluminum, glass, mixed paper, tin cans, recyclable plastics, trash, compostable food wastes, chicken stuff, etc.
- To churn butter in.
- Left-Over Paint Storage
- Pet Food Storage
- Car Wash Supplies

- Pesticide Storage
- Harmful Liquid Storage
- Pest-Proof Storage
- Sporting Goods Storage
- Charcoal Storage
- Mesquite Storage
- Dry Pool Chemicals
- Hardware Organization

Construction Industry
- Paint Storage
- Joint Compound Storage
- Nail Pail
- Tool Pail
- Dry Storage Pail
- Electrical Supplies Pail
- Electrical Cord Pail
- Hardware Organization

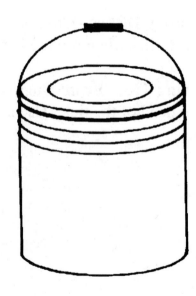

For Use In Country Living

- For storing lime next to your pot in the outhouse.
- For bringing in kindling or small logs from woodpile.
- For drying wool before weaving.
- For storing winter squash in a cool place for the winter.
- Use as a trash can.
- To reach high places with you can stand on.
- Use as a latrine.
- Plant a permanent Christmas tree in.
- For milking the cow.
- As a tote for carrying garden tools.
- For storing kindling hear wood stove.
- For bookshelf supports.
- For a step while filing horses hoofs.

General Recreational

- Tail Gate Pail/Seat
- Emergency Kit
- Dry Food Storage
- First Aid Kit
- Handy Seat

Camping

- Water-Proof Storage
- Handy Seat
- Dry Equipment Storage
- Waste Storage

Pet Industry

- Dog Food
- Horse Feed
- Bird Seed
- Rabbit Pellets
- Bulk Treats
- Aquarium Items
- Fish Transportation
- Reptile Transportation

Fishing

- Bait Pail
- Jig Pail
- Fish Storage Pail
- Tackle Pail
- Handy Seat
- Dry Equipment Storage
- Documents Storage
- First Aid Kit
- Cold Storage Pail

Emergency Preparedness

- Disaster Kits
- Food Storage
- Documents Storage

For Use Outdoors

- As a solar shower.
- As a picnic cooler.
- As a camping refrigerator.
- To pack emergency kit in trunk of car.

Resealing Solution for empty poly buckets

- Easily Re-Seals your empty poly buckets.
- Transforms your clean bucket into an airtight storage container.

This specially designed lid converts a standard 3.5 to 7 gallon plastic poly bucket into a resealable, stackable, leakproof container. Just snap on the plastic adapter to the rim of the pail, either with a small mallet or by flipping the pail over and applying pressure - then screw on the lid. Check with the supplier listed in the reference section for more information on these special lids.

Tools

Tools

One of the most important things to keep in mind when considering preparedness is having simple basic tools on hand. There are a myriad of repair jobs that are necessary for household maintenance, and this demands the right tools. It would be wise to have as many hand tools as you can afford. It would be best to obtain tools that do not need to run on gasoline or electricity, as these fuels may be unavailable in the case of a short or long term emergency.

Below we have listed various household, carpentry, mechanical and garden tools that you might want to have on hand. Many of the old-fashioned hand tools can be purchased at flea markets and garage sales. New tools can be purchased at surplus outlets and warehouse clubs.

Nails

Have several boxes of regular box nails, finishing nails and roofing nails.

Screws

Have several boxes of different size screws, including molly screws, toggle bolts and plastic anchor screws.

Saw blades

Have an extra blade available on all the different hand saws you have:

Hand saw

Hole saw

Bow saw

Metal saw

Hammers

Regular hammer

Carpenter's hammer

Screw drivers

Phillips head

Flat blade

Channel locks

Staple gun and staples

Clamps

Hand operated drill (brace & bit)

Level

Wrenchs

Pliers

Plane

Measuring Tape

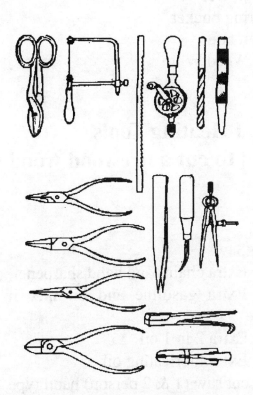

Electrical tape
Duct tape
Saw horse
Roofing repair material
    Tar paper
    Tar
    Roof Cement
Wire (different gauges)
Extra sheets of plywood and 2 x 4's (use for repair - to board up windows etc.)

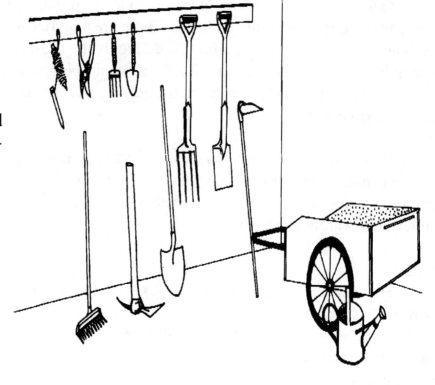

Garden Tools

Wheel barrel
Shovels
Pick
Ladder
Rakes
Hand powered lawn mower
Pitch fork
Hand trowel
Watering bucket
Garden hoe
Hand Weed Whip

Wood Heating Tools
(To cut a firewood wood supply)

Axe
Mall
Chain Saw
    Extra chains and hand sharpener
    Extra gasoline and oil mix if two cycle
engine
    Extra 2 in 1 oil
    Extra lubricating oil
Cross cut saw (1 & 2 person) hand type

Miscellaneous Tools

Paint brushes
Steel brushes
Linseed Oil
Rope
Chains
Scythe
Grinding stones
Staples
Sledge hammer
Tarps
Wire pullers
Vise
Anvil
Forge
Burlap bags
Used lumber
Used tin roofing
Washboard
Water tubs
Clothes pins
Roll roofing
Tape of all kinds
Hand or foot peddled sewing machine
Old refrigerator
Repair kits for hand water pump

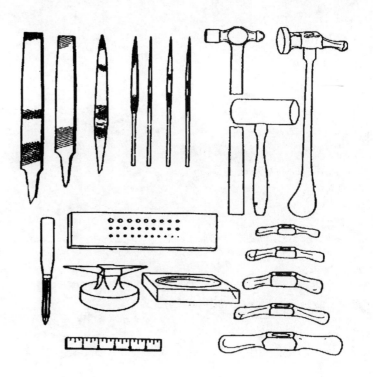

As well as keeping a supply of tools on hand, it would be wise to have a bicycle on hand as well. A bicycle will be an excellent vehicle (preferably a mountain bike) if for some reason gasoline were unavailable for automobiles. If you were to keep extra bicycle parts on hand such as tubes, tires, spokes, rims and tube patch kits, you would be able to do your own repairs if necessary.

There are many books on the market that show you how to do basic plumbing, electrical and carpentry repairs to your home. Some of these are *Back to Basics* by Reader's Digest and *Simple Home Repairs* by Storey Communications, Inc.

Homesteading

Suburban Homestead

This graphic design of a suburban setting was created by Kristan Johnson of Abundant Landscape Design in Seattle Washington (206) 522-3663. This is an excellent example of what a family living in or near the city can do with their home and property to prepare for a sovereign lifestyle. In the event that you cannot afford to purchase and maintain a rural retreat property, or move to a rural area, you can use this idealized picture to help you plan for the future. Most of these plants can be obtain from Raintree Nursery in Morton, Washington, (206) 496-6400.

Let's take an imaginary walk around this property. Follow the numbers as a guide and refer to the above picture.

1.   Newly laid brick pathway
2.   Front porch
3.   Small fir forest in upper left hand corner, also interplanted with saskatoon serviceberry, red-twigged dogwood, evergreen huckleberry and salal.
4.   Path bordered by daylilies, lingonberries and wintergreen
5.   Red-leafed plum tree
6.   Siberian pea shrub in the background

7.	Overhead trellis of grapes on the front porch.
8.	Espaliered apple and pears.
9.	Up front is a rippling pond
10.	Strawberry tree with red fruit
11.	Planting of asparagus
12.	Border of ground cover bamboo.
13.	Planting of artichokes
14.	Dwarf peach and nectarine trees
15.	Firepit area.
16.	Cascading strawberries
17.	Weeping Santa Rosa Plum.
18.	Blueberry hedge
19.	Gooseberries
21	Wood storage area.
22.	Prolific kiwis trellised along garage.
23	Littleleaf Linden
24	Woodlot of red alder, black locust, maple and chestnut for firewood.
26	Mushroom garden
27	Old Chestnut tree for quiet meditation
28.	Shade lilac
29.	Highbush cranberry
30.	Rosa Rugosa
31.	Kitchen herb garden
32.	Back deck
33.	Citrus plants grown in portable containers
34.	Evergreen huckleberry hedge
35.	Espaliered fig tree.

You could possibly survive if you were unable to leave the city in the event of a short or long-term emergency, though leaving the cities would be ideal. Use this above picture as an idea for planting your property for future food resources and wood burning potential. There are many different ways to approach this, depending upon the layout of your home and property. Be creative and design your layout to your specific requirements and needs.

Cheese

Cheese is the product of milk that has been curdled. Milk curdles when the enzyme rennin is added. There are two types of cheese: soft and hard. Soft cheeses are made from unpressed curds. These must be eaten within a few weeks. Hard cheeses take longer to prepare but keep much longer. In fact, when cheese has developed a skin on its surface, it can be kept for a long time in a cool dry place.

Cow's milk is the most popular base for cheese. Goat's milk cheese is mild when fresh but may develop a strong ammonia taste if kept for too long. Roquefort cheese is made from sheep's milk. Rich and creamy cheeses are made from whole raw milk. Reconstituted dry milk can also be used for cheese recipes. If you are using pasteurized milk however, you should add some buttermilk as a cheese starter.

Rennet, the substance that contains the rennin needed to curdle milk, is available in most pharmacies and specialty stores. Dried pieces of calves or lambs stomach also has the rennin enzyme in it and can be used to curdle milk.

To make cheese you need certain tools. These tools are a 4 - 5 gallon pot which will nestle inside a larger pot, to act as a double boiler, a dairy thermometer, a long knife for slicing the curdled milk, a large ladle and several yards of cheesecloth. A cylindrical mold or cheese press is also useful for the final product.

Making Cheese

To make a hard cheese you need to have ripened milk. One gallon of milk will make about 1 1/2 to 2 pounds of cheese. If you use raw milk take half from fresh milk in the morning and half from last evening's milk that has stood at room temperature all night. If pasteurized milk is used, heat it in a double boiler to 86°F and stir in a cup of unpasteurized buttermilk per each gallon of pasteurized milk. Let stand for 30 minutes to 3 hours depending upon how sharp you want your cheese to taste.

Draining curds for cottage cheese

Once the milk is ready add rennet to curdle it. Rennet tablets are sold for cheese making. Use one eighth of a cheese rennet tablet per gallon of milk. Dissolve the rennet in 30 to 40 times its volume of cool water before putting into the milk. Stir the milk and rennet solution thoroughly and place in a warm location. After 45 minutes a thin layer of watery

129

1   Leave milk overnight. Separate cream

2   Add morning's milk. Heat to 92°F.

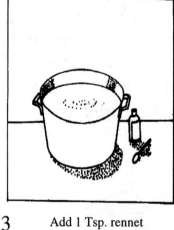

3   Add 1 Tsp. rennet

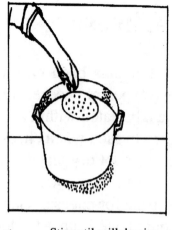

4   Stir until milk begins to cling.

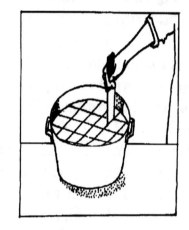

5   When curds firm, cut with knife.

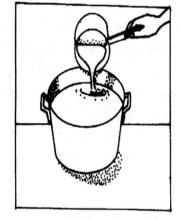

6   Warm whey and add to curds.

whey will appear on top with firm custard-like curds beneath. Cut the curds immediately, as they will soon begin to deteriorate. Slice the curds into even-sized cubes so they will all cook at the same speed. Mix the cut curds for 10 minutes, then start to heat the curds and whey very slowly. If heated too quickly they become tough on the outside but are watery inside. Stir gently to avoid crushing them.

After the curds are cooked, strain off the whey and mix in 3 tsp. of salt per gallon of milk. Put the curds in the cheese press, apply gentle pressure for the first hour or two to avoid bruising them. Gradually add more weight, thus a harder cheese is created over time. After the cheese has been pressed, allow it to dry in a cool, airy place for 4 - 5 days. Turn it over twice each day. Finally, coat the cheese with paraffin, butter, vegetable oil, or salt to allow it to ripen in a cool, well-ventilated area. Cheese will improve in flavor for several months. Date your cheese, making a note of any special methods you used.

Powdered Milk Cheese

If you only have powdered milk to use you can substitute this for cow's, goats or sheep's milk. Use 1 part water to 1/2 part powdered or instant milk. For example: 4 cups water to 2 cups powdered milk. Boil milk and then cool to 86°F. Dissolve rennet into warm water and add milk. Proceed as with the above recipe for the final cheese product.

Making Butter

Butter is made from the cream that rises to the top of milk. If you allow the cream to ripen it churns more rapidly and produces more flavor in the butter. It is the butterfat that is suspended in the cream that makes butter. The churning process is what helps to coagulate the butterfat and turn the cream into butter.

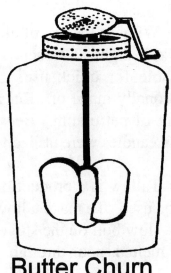

Butter Churn

For best results the cream should be at about 60°F before churning. If you churn at a higher temperature the butter will be soft and keep poorly. If you churn at a much lower temperature the butter will take much longer to form.

If you don't have a butter churn you can simply agitate the cream in a covered jar. A good butter churn is worth owning if you can find one. After 15 minutes of churning the cream should begin to feel heavy. After another 10 to 20 minutes the cream should separate into buttermilk and grain-sized pellets of butter. Once the granules have formed, stop churning, drain the buttermilk from the churn and rinse the butter with cold water. Work the butter granules together with a butter paddle or wooden spoon. You can add salt at this time - 1/4 to 1/2 tsp. per pound of butter. Unsalted butter spoils quickly. Wrap in wax paper and place in a freezer, refrigerator, spring house or the coolest place you have.

CANDLE MAKING

Without the use of electric power it will be essential to have some form of lighting for use at night. Kerosene or oil lamps are useful, but it is always handy to have candles available for quick use. There are a number of materials that candles have been traditionally made of. Beeswax and tallow were the only materials available before the advent of petroleum. Beeswax was considered the candle source for the wealthy and tallow candles were utilized by the poor.

Tallow is a product of animal fat. Beef fat is considered good, but sheep fat can also be used. To make tallow simply take the fat that is left over from butchering and bring it to a slow boil on the stove. A low fire keeps it from burning or smoking. When the fat is all melted, pour through a cloth or cheesecloth filter. This will filter out the animal parts and purify the fat. The fat is then cooled and used to make either drip or mold candles.

Beeswax is a scarcer commodity. If you can obtain some comb honey, first separate the honey from the comb. Take the comb and combine it with two cups of water and place in a pan over a low heat. The water will keep the beeswax from catching on fire. When it is thoroughly melted pour it through a cloth or cheesecloth, as with rendering the tallow. This will separate out any impurities and make a smoother consistency. Beeswax can be added to tallow or paraffin to make a stronger and better smelling candle.

Paraffin is a petroleum by-product. It comes in different grades for different hardness in the finished candle. For a firmer, brighter-burning candle add 3 tablespoons of powdered stearin per pound of paraffin. Stearin is generally available at a candle supply store.

Wicks are the fuel of a candle. A good wick will blot up the molten wax, provide a surface for the wax to burn on, and not burn up too quickly itself. To make your own wicks you can soak heavy cotton yarn for 12 hours in a solution of 1 Tbs. of salt plus 2 Tbs. of boric acid in a cup of water. After the yarn is dry, braid three strands together to form the wick. Too large a wick will cause a smoky candle; too small a wick and the flame will be doused in melted wax.

Making Molded Candles

There are many containers that can serve as a mold for candles. Milk cartons, jars, cans, plastic cups, cardboard rolls and many other common containers. Coat the interior of each mold with cooking oil or silicone spray to prevent sticking. Waxed containers need not be coated. If the mold is cardboard wrap a string around it so that it will hold its shape during the process. Place your wick in the container and affix it to the bottom of the container with putty or even tape. Use a coffee can for melting your wax. Heat the wax to 130ºF for cardboard, plastic or glass molds; 190ºF for metal molds. Pour wax into the mold and let it sit overnight, then refrigerate for 12 hours. Dip glass or metal into hot water to release the mold. Other than manufactured candle molds, homemade molds are easy to use. Be sure that the opening of a homemade mold is larger than its base or else the candle will not be released.

Making Dipped Candles

Two cans will be needed for candle dipping - one to hold the molten wax, the other to hold cool water. The cans should be taller than the candles you wish to make. Heat molten wax to 150 - 180ºF during the dipping procedure. The water in the cool can should be room temperature.

Cut wicks 4 inches longer than the finished candle. Tie a nail or washer to the lower end for weight. You can dip individually or tie the candles to a dowel and dip in a row. First dip the wicks into the molten wax then place them in the cool water. Continue to repeat this process until the desired thickness of candle is reached. It may take from 30 to 40 dippings to get a candle 1 inch in diameter.

To harden the wax around the outer layer of candle add a tablespoon of stearin to the molten wax for the final dipping. After the dipping is finished trim the wicks, leaving 1/2 inch on each end.

If you plan on making candles in the future it would be a good idea to stock up on supplies while they are still available.

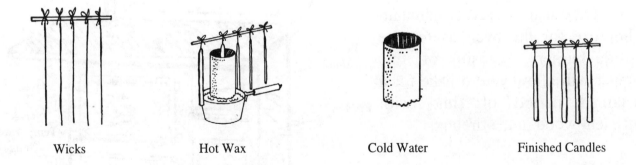

Wicks   Hot Wax   Cold Water   Finished Candles

WOODSTOVE COOKERY

The ideal solution to having hot food and water when the electric power is out is to have a wood cook stove. This particular stove is ideal because it only relies on wood - no need for propane, electricity or even solar power. A wood cook stove will also help to warm the house in the colder months. Most peoples grandmother was either raised with or cooked on a wood cook stove. They can burn either coal or wood. Though they can be tricky to learn to use, once you are familiar with gauging the temperature of the stove and controlling the firebox heat, you can cook anything you desire.

To understand a wood cook stove you need to know what its parts are and how to use them. The area where fuel is consumed and heat is produced is the firebox. This is usually underneath the cooking lids and beside the oven. Forming the base of the firebox is the grate. This is what supports the fuel and allows the ashes to fall below. The ashbox below the grate can be removed and emptied easily.

Below the firebox or to the side of it is the draft control. The draft allows you to control the amount of air that flows to the fire in the firebox. Controlling the amount of air determines how hot the fire is. If you allow a lot of air to reach the fire and keep adding fuel you will get a very hot fire. If you close off the draft and starve the fire for air, the fire will eventually cool down. Controlling the air can also determine how long the fire burns. When you have established a nice hot fire and wish to add a good size log and maintain the fire, you close down the draft control and let the fire stabilize.

The oven can be controlled by adjusting the stovepipe damper. The same mechanism is used to maintain a hot fire for the oven as for the topside burners. Closing off this damper will allow you to bake for a sustained period of time with sufficient wood in the firebox.

On the top of most stoves is a warming oven. This is where you can put bread while it is rising, or food to keep warm until serving.

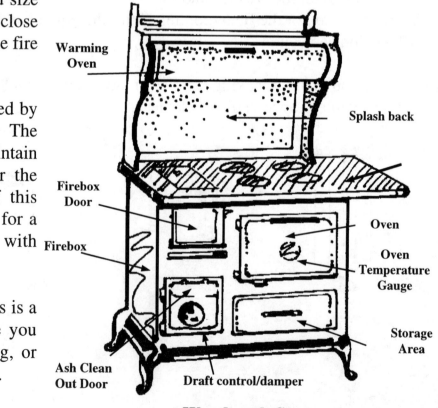

Wood cook Stove

134

Creating a fire in the firebox is essentially the same as starting a fire in any wood burning stove. You begin in stages and build up to a good sustained fire. Avoid the temptation to keep one of the lid covers off so that you can watch the fire build - this spoils the draft and lets all the heat escape. If you must check on the fire do so from the side dampers of the firebox. Ultimately you are going to have to experiment until you get used to your stove. Though the technique is essentially the same, all wood burning stoves are unique and must be worked with to get a good long burning fire.

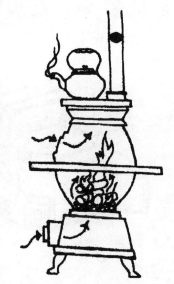

You should also familiarize yourself with the different types of wood used for wood burning. Soft woods such as pine, cedar and redwood are good for kindling and help to get a fire going quickly. But to sustain a good long burning fire you need to add hard woods to the hot coals you have created in the initial stages. Oak, larch, maple and Douglas fir are good woods to add to the fire to keep it hot. You will also have to experiment with different sizes of wood that will be ideal for the size of your firebox.

Most regular wood or coal space heaters or stoves have at least one or more surfaces that can be used to cook on. Even a fireplace can be used to cook food. A pot of hot soup or stew is a great comforter in tough times.

Hot Water

It is possible to have a large quantity of hot water, even though you may not have any electrical back-up devices to run a water heater or have a propane water heater. The picture to the right shows how you can heat a 55 gallon drum that has been laid on its side. As shown, the side has been drilled and a siphon is then inserted at one end. A funnel is inserted to another hole in the other end to pour in the water to be heated. When the water is at sufficient temperature you simply siphon it out the opposite end. This is one way to get a hot bath or get a lot of water to wash clothes. Experiment on your own with different size containers placing them over a source of heat or open pit fire.

Harvesting Firewood

Collecting your own wood burning fuel from the woods can be a very satisfying effort. It is healthful and vigorous exercise to move from felling a tree to splitting and stacking the wood. A good day's work will harvest a cord of wood.

An efficient chain saw is a necessary tool for felling and bucking (cutting) up a tree. You can also use a two-man saw for this purpose and it would be good to have one on hand in the event you could not get parts or fuel for the chain saw. It is also wise to store extra chain saw blades, 2 in 1 oil and gasoline for a time when these commodities may be unavailable. Also, be sure to keep your chain saw blades sharp. A dull chain saw not only requires much more labor but it can be hazardous. You can tell when your blade is dull if the chips become smaller, more force is required to make the saw cut the wood and the wood smokes due to increased friction.

Felling A Tree

(See the diagram on the right) To properly notch a tree for felling, make the first notch on the side facing the desired direction of fall. This requires two cuts, an undercut, then a face cut. A third cut is made slightly above and

← Direction of Fall

Wrap a long rope around upper trunk and pull to start fall. Be careful and be far away

Second Cut
Face cut

First Cut
undercut

Third Cut

behind the first notch as shown. If a tree does not fall of its own accord, you push it from behind with a pole or you can have a pulley set up which will pull it in the right direction.

Felling a tree can be dangerous. If any part of the tree is rotten it may twist or bounce off another tree or kick back and fall in the opposite direction. For this reason it is vital to have at least one, preferably, two clear escape routes and get out of the way as soon as the tree begins to fall.

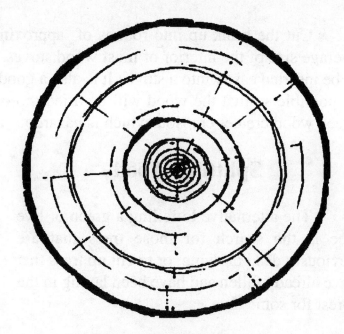

Tree Cross Section

Winter is the easiest time to fell trees. It is easier to spot dead trees, to choose a safe path of fall and to plan a good escape route.

When you have felled a tree, the first thing to do is to remove the limbs. When you are removing a limb from a felled tree stand on the opposite side of the trunk. This will minimize the risk of cutting your foot with the saw or axe. Be aware of whether the limb you are removing is in any way supporting the tree above the ground. If it is and you remove it, the tree may shift suddenly and knock you off your balance.

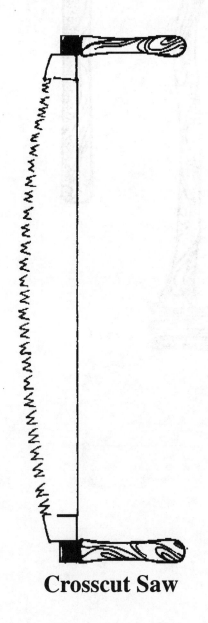

Crosscut Saw

When the weight of a tree is suspended over a hollow space beneath, realize that cutting into the log will cause it to fall down and compress against the chain saw blade. To avoid the blade being pinched and stuck you should first make an undercut up to one third the diameter of the log on the bottom side of the trunk. Then cut from the top. In this way you will have the tree cut through before the pinching process would lock the blade into the trunk. If the chain saw does bind, put a wedge into the cut and pry it apart, releasing the blade.

Cut the trunk up into rounds of approximately 18 inches in length. This is the average size of the interior of most wood stoves. This is a comfortable size for the logs to be inserted easily into a stove. It is also a good idea to split what you have cut as soon as possible so that the wood will be dried thoroughly before burning. Burning wet or green wood creates creosote which is hazardous and may cause a chimney fire.

Splitting Wood

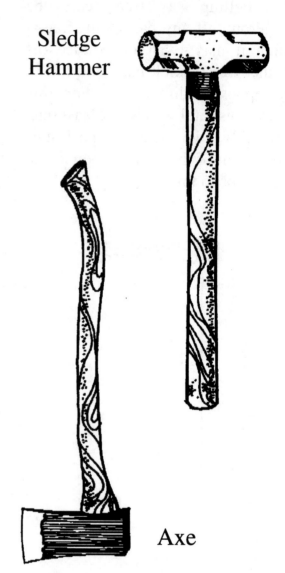

Sledge
Hammer

Axe

The alternative to felling a green or live tree is the search for those trees that are obviously dead or dying, or to cut up trees that have already fallen and have been laying in the forest for some time.

There are numerous varieties of trees that are superior for wood burning stoves. Pine and cedar are softwoods that dry quickly and are good for kindling and starting the fire. They burn quickly so they are not good for producing a sustained fire. Oak, Larch, Douglas fir and Maple are superior woods for a long sustained hot fire. These are hardwoods that are dense and burn for a long time, creating a very hot fire. Regular Fir, Alder, Cottonwood and Redwood are medium woods. The price of firewood depends upon whether it is a softwood or hardwood. Hardwood cords sell for more. A cord of wood is approximately 4' x 4' x 8'.

Animals for Self-Sufficiency

There are a number of animals that you can raise that will provide you with all the meat, eggs, milk, cheese, butter and wool that you might want. If there were a sizeable economic collapse, or natural disaster, these commodities would be impossible to obtain from a supermarket. Therefore, you should consider raising several different animals to meet these needs.

We do not desire to go into great detail here on the raising and care of domestic animals. What we would like to do, as with the rest of this book, is introduce you to these concepts and give you enough information so that you can begin to prepare yourself for self-reliant living. If you do obtain different animals for use in a rural setting you should get some of the reference material we will provide at the end of this section. Caring for animals is a serious responsibility and should not be attempted without first making the commitment to proper care and having adequate facilities to do so.

Remember that in the future feed for any animals you own will have to be provided from your own land. Therefore, you need adequate pasture land, and should be able to grow your own supplemental grains. It is also necessary to provide some kind of shelter for most animals. If you are living in an urban setting your zoning requirements may prohibit this. If you are considering purchasing rural property, take these requirements into account when deciding which property to purchase.

It is highly possible that the services of a good veterinarian will be impossible to obtain during either a short or long term emergency situation. It would be wise to familiarize yourself with what medications, herbal, or homeopathic remedies are necessary to maintaining healthy animals. Each species has its own special needs.

The following will be a thumbnail sketch of the basic requirements for shelter and health of certain animals. Hopefully, with this information you can then decide which animals would be appropriate for your situation. Animals are a wonderful addition to any homestead. They not only provide products but they can be very affectionate and delightful to have around.

Bees

If you love honey and want fresh honey as opposed to storing enough, consider keeping bees. Once you have them set up with a good hive, bees are little or no maintenance. They actually prefer to be left alone. Another benefit of having bees is that they will pollinate your fruit trees and entire garden each year.

To raise bees you need a standard hive. This includes a brood chamber where the bees live and raise their young; supers (where the honey is stored); frames and wax foundation to insert into the hive and supers; and a smoker to calm the bees when you are working with them. You should also purchase a good veil and long gloves to prevent being stung while opening the hive and working with the bees.

Have a place where the hive will get sun in the morning and shade in the afternoon. It should be sheltered from strong winds and away from human traffic. Bees also need a source of fresh water somewhere in the vicinity, such as a bird bath or a small pool.

Honey yields will vary from each hive. You need to leave some of the honey for the bees to use during the winter. What is left over for you can be anywhere from nothing to possibly 200 pounds or more of honey. Bee keeping can be risky in very cold climates. If the hive freezes during a hard winter the entire swarm of bees is lost. You need to provide a place to shelter the hive in harsh climates.

Bee keeping is not for everyone, but it can provide a fresh supply of good honey if you want to invest the money and are not concerned with being close to bees.

Chickens

Chickens are well known as a provider of eggs. Eggs are a source of high quality protein, particularly fertilized eggs. If you have several hens and a rooster you can have you own fresh supply of eggs year round. They are little trouble and don't demand a lot of feed or attention. Chickens are a definite consideration for self-reliant living.

There are several species that are known for prolific egg production. These are White Leghorn, Barred or White Rocks and Rhode Island Reds. Leghorns lay a white egg and the Rocks and Reds lay brown eggs. Feed a high protein ration for about six months, then switch to a lower protein, high calcium feed and you can expect one egg every other day from each hen.

If you want to have your own food on hand in the future you can plant corn and dry it to produce scratch. It might be a good idea to store a bag or two of crushed oyster shells. This will supply added calcium to the diet and create a harder shell on the eggs. Chickens are very good at eating whatever you would normally throw into a compost pile from your own kitchen table scraps. Chickens that are allowed to free range, or run freely on the property, will also supplement their diet with grass, worms and insects.

Chickens also provide meat. There are particular breeds that are used for meat, these are a cross between a White Cornish male and a White Rock female. It takes several months for these crosses to reach seven or eight pounds, suitable for roasting. One chicken that is able to produce a sizeable number of eggs and retain a fair amount of fat for roasting is the Rhode Island Red. Since roosters don't produce eggs they can be processed into meat within the first six months of growth. If you wait to eat them until after six months, roosters can become tough and you would need a pressure canner to tenderize the meat.

Chickens should have some kind of housing or a coop as it is called. A chicken coop is also desirable so that they can get out of the weather. They prefer to a have a closed space, such as a box, to lay eggs in. Something that has three sides and preferably a top to it. Chickens also love to roost or to have available to them a large branch or rod that they can sit on at night. Chickens are birds and have most of the same habits that birds in the wild do. If you are unable to supplement their feed they will search for it and they like to go up onto the branches of trees to rest. Turkeys, ducks and geese are similar to chickens in their ability lay eggs and provide meat.

Cattle

Cattle are an animal to consider if you like beef products and enjoy cow's milk. You need a good barn and at least two acres per cow if you are to successfully raise cows for meat or dairy products. A cow also needs to be bred once a year to produce milk. It is a lactating mother that produces milk. Therefore, you need to have an availability of artificial insemination or a bull to keep with a cow.

Cows, like sheep and goats, are ruminants. This means that they can absorb nutrients from grasses and leaves. Since you would most likely be keeping a cow for milk production you need to provide a pasture that is rich in legumes, clover or alfalfa. You also need to have sufficient pasture and to rotate the cows between at least two areas to prevent overgrazing.

During winter months cows needs to be fed supplemental hay. A cow needs at least 2 to 3 pounds of hay per 100 pounds of body weight. An average milking cow will weigh approximately 1,200 lbs. Grains such as ground corn, oats, barley and wheat bran should supplement the diet of a lactating cow. Cows also need a salt lick and a fresh supply of water available to them at all times.

It must be remembered that a milking cow needs to be milked daily. This must be done twice a day at 12 hour intervals. You also need to keep their barn area clean. They are a large animal and can be intimidating unless you are used to working with them. Because they are a large animal they need a fairly good sized barn to provide shelter and a regular milking area.

Goats

Goats are an animal to consider if you are allergic to cow's milk and would like to have milk in your diet. Goat's milk is slightly higher in calcium than cow's milk. One goat can produce up to 3 to 4 quarts of milk per day. Goat's milk can be easier to digest than cow's milk because it is naturally homogenized - the fat particles are so small they do not separate from the rest of the milk. Butter and cheese can be made from goat's milk, but you need to purchase certain breeds of goat to get a high butterfat content.

Goats tend to be browsers as opposed to grazers. This means that they are fond of foliage or tree branches for their food. Therefore a goat's pasture needs to include leaves, branches, weeds and tough grasses. Goats will not eat hay or supplemental feed placed on the ground. It must be paced in a manger or hung in bundles. A milking doe needs extra grain each day and molasses added to the water. The molasses provides the extra calcium and minerals necessary for lactating. Overfeeding of grain can be dangerous. In fact, any grain stored needs to be inaccessible to the goats. Goats as with sheep can overeat and cause themselves severe to fatal digestive problems. Plenty of fresh clean water is essential for any milk producing animal.

Goats need shelter from the weather and a place where you can comfortably milk them. A milking stand should be created in the shelter area for the goats to feed at while they are being milked. Their sleeping area should be draft free and they like a lot of hay to bed in.

Goats need adequate fencing. They are precocious and always looking for new delicacies to eat. They can destroy flimsy fencing and will devour your garden if it is not properly protected. They can jump fairly high and will do so if there is something they want. Many people tether their goats in specific areas to keep them from the produce garden. This tethering should be rotated to provide adequate exercise and foraging.

Goats can be very affectionate and act as a pet, similar to having a dog. Many people enjoy the personality of goats. Goats are bright and can outwit you if they aren't challenged. If you have the time and the patience to spend on goats they can be a delightful addition to any homestead.

Horses

Horses can provide work, mobility and pleasure for a homesteader. However, they are a high maintenance animal and careful consideration should be given to owning a horse. If you are considering a future where you will be unable to obtain a veterinarian or purchase supplemental hay or grain, you must have enough land to provide adequate pasture and sufficient shelter for a horse.

Horses have delicate stomachs and must be fed carefully. If you are working a horse you need to supplement pasturage with oats and other grain. Wheat bran and corn are other supplemental feeds. Each horse needs between 2 to 3 acres for the pasture to be adequate in size. This pasture should have a combination of clover and alfalfa. Horses can consume between 8 to 12 pounds per day of hay if you can only feed supplemental. They also need a fresh supply of water at all times and a salt lick or mineral cube.

Your need for a horse will determine the kind of breed you would choose. There are horses specifically bred for working and some for riding. Talk to a local horse breeder for adequate information on breeds and their uses. In fact, it would be highly recommended that you spend some time around horses, if you haven't already done so, before you decide to invest the time, land and money into a horse.

Horses needs good shelter, preferably some kind of barn where they have a stall of their own. A barn is also necessary to store any supplemental hay or grain for future use. Horses also require special harnesses, bridles or saddles if you prefer one and other equipment unique to their care. They also need to be shod (have their horseshoes replaced) regularly. You should have the equipment and knowledge to do this yourself. Knowing that a veterinarian may be unavailable for future use you need to familiarize yourself with their potential health problems and have the necessary medications stored.

Horses are a large responsibility, they need a lot of attention, and should be ridden often for proper care. Though they require a larger area than most animals and special equipment, they are a valuable addition to any homestead.

Pigs

Some people would like to have pork added to their diet. If this is the case they need to keep one or two pigs on hand. Though pigs have earned a poor reputation in the past they are considered to be very intelligent animals.

The meat obtainable from pigs is ham, roast pork, chops, sausage and bacon. Their lard or fat is also usable. Pigs need little space and don't demand elaborate surroundings. They can be fed the kitchen table scraps. It is felt that they require the least time and work for the amount of meat produced.

Again, if you live in an urban area you need to check your zoning requirements, as they are not welcome in all neighborhoods. Pigs need an area where they can eat grass and dig in the cool earth. Of course, this should be at a distance from your home since they are known for their permeating aroma.

Fencing for a pig must be a 3 foot well-anchored woven wire fence. A board or metal needs to be extended into the ground as they attempt to dig themselves out. They are forever attempting to leave the pen. Pigs also need to be protected from wandering coyotes or wolves. There should be some form of shelter with roosts available to get them out of harsh weather.

To fatten pigs for food there are many commercial supplements available. They are expensive however, and often contain hormones that are toxic to humans. If you are wanting to have pork in the future, you will need to feed your pigs from your own table scraps and grain that you might grow yourself or have stored. Pigs need fresh water available at all times. They also love the extra milk or buttermilk from any milking animal.

Rabbits

Rabbits can be good source of protein for eating and they take up relatively little space. It is felt that a rabbit will produce more high protein meat per dollar of feed than any other animal. If you are growing rabbit for meat it is best to keep them in a confined area, either specific cages or a well wired pen. Rabbits that are kept on the ground have a funny habit of digging deeply under the fencing and getting free. Once they are free they will ravage the garden and be very hard to catch.

Rabbits can be fed grain, grass clippings and vegetable tops or fruit tree leaves. Fresh water is essential and a salt lick available at all times. You need not store any special feed for rabbits, such as commercial pellets, unless you choose to.

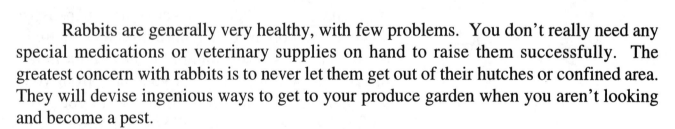

Another benefit of rabbits is that they are prolific breeders. Does (female rabbits) are almost continuously fertile. You only need one buck and one doe to begin with to have a steady supply of rabbit meat for the future. The male rabbit does need to be separated from a new mother with baby rabbits, as they have a tendency to eat the babies.

Rabbits are generally very healthy, with few problems. You don't really need any special medications or veterinary supplies on hand to raise them successfully. The greatest concern with rabbits is to never let them get out of their hutches or confined area. They will devise ingenious ways to get to your produce garden when you aren't looking and become a pest.

Sheep

Sheep are a definite consideration for a self-reliant lifestyle. They can provide meat, wool, tallow for candles and even milk for dairy products. Sheep's milk is very high in butter fat. Sheep are a herd animal so it is best to obtain at least three. You can raise them on less than five acres. They are very low maintenance and require only nominal shelter from the weather.

Sheep are ruminants, having four stomachs, and provide most of their nutrition from pasture grass. If you are able you should supplement a pregnant ewe's (female sheep) diet with alfalfa. A pregnant ewe also needs molasses in her water to add extra calcium for lactating. Therefore, you might need to store extra molasses for future use. Sheep need a salt lick available at all times and fresh water.

For shelter sheep can get by with just a lean-to to get out of the rain. It is advisable though to give them a small barn or shelter area where lambing ewes can give birth. Sheep should be sheared once a year, not only to obtain the valuable wool, but to relieve them of their wool in hot weather. Therefore, you need to know how to do this and have the proper shears on hand for future use.

Sheep have relatively few medical problems, short of digestive problems. As with goats, sheep have been known to over eat, therefore any supplemental grain needs to be stored where they cannot get to it. Also, if their pasture or feed is changed too radically they can get bloated, which can result in death.

Sheep are relatively maintenance free and they are very nice creatures to have around. They are friendly, but not invasive of the garden if it is adequately fenced. They don't tend to roam from their property unless they don't have enough to eat. Lambs are probably the cutest creatures around to have as an addition to any homestead. They are full of energy and their antics are a source of good entertainment. Sheep are recommended as an excellent animal for self-reliant living because they provide so many different products and are so easy to keep.

Reference Material for Further Reading

Bees: The Art and Adventure of Beekeeping by Harry Aebi
First Lessons in Beekeeping, by C. P Dadant
The Complete Guide to Beekeeping, by Roger A. Morse

Chickens: Eggs and Chickens by John Vivian - Storey Publishing

Cattle: Raising a Calf for Beef by Phyllis Hobson

Goats: Raising Milk Goats the Modern Way by Jerry Belanger

Horses: Horse Sense by John J. Mettler, Jr.
Your Horse, by Judy Chapple

Pigs: Small-Scale Pig Raising By Dirk van Loon

Rabbits: Raising Rabbits the Modern Way by Bob Bennett

Sheep: Raising Sheep the Modern Way by Paula Simmons

Alternative Energy

Alternative Energy

In the event of a natural or economic disaster it is highly likely that electricity will be unavailable for either a short or long period of time. If you are heavily dependent on electrical devices to run your household and appliances, you need to consider alternative sources of energy as a back up.

We will give a brief explanation of what electricity is and how it is measured. In this way you will understand what it is you are converting. Electricity is the flow of electrons through a conductor, or analogously the flow of water through a pipe. The pressure with which the electrons flow through a given size pipe is called the voltage. The greater the pressure the faster the flow. The rate of flow or speed of the electrons is the amperage. The size of conductor or wire determines the amount of electricity or amperage that is allowed to flow for a given voltage.

The wattage of electricity is determined by multiplying the voltage by the amperes. Therefore, electrical power or wattage is a function of the pressure (voltage) and amount (amperage). Most electrical appliances and conduction systems are measured in watts. A kilowatt is one thousand watts of power. Watts is the amount of work being done to perform whatever task is required, i.e. light a 75 watt bulb.

There are two kinds of current, DC or direct current and AC or alternating current. Direct current simply flows in one direction at all times. Alternating current flows in one direction for a period of time and then reverses direction for the same period of time. AC current creates a wave form that is measured in Hertz (Hz) or cycles per second. So 60 Hertz is a sixty cycle per second current flow.

Whether you decide to use a generator, or any other form of alternative energy, you will need to calculate the power consumption you currently use, and what you think you will use in an emergency situation. This load is determined by the watt-hours of power. A one watt load that is powered for one hour will consume one watt-hour of power. A 100 watt load powered for 2 hours will consume 200 watt-hours, etc. To determine your watt-hours you need to take the wattage of the appliance or fixture used, and multiply by the number of hours a day that you use it, in order to determine watt-hours. Total the number of watt-hours for each appliance used in a day to determine the total power consumption per day.

Any <u>home</u> electrical system is going to have three components: a transmission system, a storage system (batteries) and a voltage regulation system. Electricity is produced by solar panels, wind, hydro or a fuel driven generator and then stored in batteries. There are several kinds of batteries, the most common being lead/acid, nickel-cadmium or gel-cell batteries. There are various advantages and disadvantages of using the different types of batteries for back-up electrical power.

The depth of charge is important if you are considering solar power. Depth of charge is measured by how much of the battery's power can be discharged and then recharged, without damaging them or reducing their life. Twenty percent or less is considered a shallow cycle and is typical of automobile batteries. If eighty percent of the battery capacity can be discharged and recharged this is a deep cycle battery. Since solar demands you keep constant watch on your battery consumption, deep cycle batteries are more efficient to use.

The kinds of batteries you purchase for your electrical system will depend on what appliances you want to run and for how long. Look in the reference section following this chapter for the material you can study to make this determination.

A fuel driven (gas, propane, natural gas, etc.) generator is a good idea for an electric back-up device. It will keep batteries recharged and run small appliances and power tools. There are many kinds and sizes of generators on the market, depending upon how extensively you want to use this type of back up system.

All generators have magnets of one kind or another. One kind is the electromagnet, which has wires wrapped around an iron core. If an electric current is passed through the wire, the assembly becomes magnetized. Another kind uses permanent magnets. Permanent magnets are made of special materials that have been passed through a magnetic field and perpetually retain their magnetism. An electric current is produced when a conductor passes through a magnetic field. The wire conductors are called armatures. The fundamental rule of electric generators is the electricity that is created by a the relationship between the armatures and the magnetic fields.

Generators come in various sizes and capacities. Some act as a simple alternator, such as the alternator in your car, which produces low voltage electricity. Some are permanent magnet rotor motors which produce high voltages. The following chart will give you an idea of the difference between generators. (PM = permanent magnet)

Generator	Cost	Efficiency	Reliability	Output Voltage Adjustment
Alternator	low	low	high	easy
PM Stator motor	medium	high	medium	very complex
PM Rotor motor	high	high	high	fairly easy

A 4,000 watt generator will run a well pump, the lights and small appliances for a small house. When purchasing a generator you should consider whether it has a 220 volt outlet, in case your well pump is 220 volts, and also if it runs on diesel or regular fuel. Your best source of information on generators is to go to dealers and compare the various products on the market. You need to realize that this is essentially only a back up device. Most generators are not designed for long term continuous use. You cannot run either an electric stove or a hot water heater with a generator of this size. A bigger generator is very costly and expensive to run, but that is your choice. Generators are great for back-up of a complete solar electric system to keep the batteries charged when the sun isn't shining. Some generators are called dual fuel which means they will run on either gas, propane or natural gas. This type will give you more options on fuel.

It is also a good idea to have your well pump, a light circuit and any other device pre-wired with a pigtail adapter that can be attached to your generator in the event of an emergency. **Please remember you are dealing with potentially dangerous high voltages. A licensed electrician should be hired to do this for you.** The ends of the pigtail adapter need to be sealed when not in use. In some cases breakers or fuses need to be turned off when using your generator in this manner. This avoids feeding electricity back through your system and preventing possible damage when the power comes back on. It is simple once you understand, but again, have a competent licensed electrician set this up for you.

When you are running power tools from a generator you need to use a heavy duty extension cord from the generator to the power tool. If the extension cord is too small, you risk burning out the tool you are using.

Propane is another alternative energy source. Purchase some propane appliances for emergency use. As a

Typical Solar System

Typical Stationary Solar Panel Array

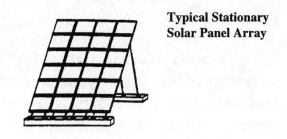

Wiring to Array

Remote Metering

AC Distribution

Battery Enclosure (Vented)

Inverters

you can purchase a small metal baking box that sits on a heat source like a portable propane camp stove, wood heater, etc. These are small and relatively inexpensive and can be stored easily when not in use. If you have a full propane tank stored for emergency use you can quickly connect the stove to the tank and have instant cooking. Propane cylinders have a long shelf life and can be stored in a small space.

If you live in an area with good year-round sun, then solar energy can be used as a main or alternative source of electrical power. Many people build their homes, and never hook up to the local electrical grid. If a proper solar energy system is created in the building stages, or added on to an existing house, you can run a number of electrical appliances, lighting, water pump and power tools on the solar panel system. You must weigh the advantages and disadvantages of paying up-front for a costly solar system against having your own power for many years to come, at relatively low cost and maintenance.

A Solar Electric Generating System may not be for everyone. The greatest advantage of purchasing your own solar system is freedom from the utility company. If you own your own system you will be free from increased rate changes and power outages. Most solar systems last from between 25 - 50 years. You can run most electric equipment depending on system size, including refrigerator, freezer, lights, water pump and hand powered tools. For example, if you paid $15,000 for a system and it lasts X years (see chart) your payout would look like this:

Year	Cost/Yr.	Cost/Mo.	Cost/Day
15 yrs.	$1,000	$83.33	$2.78
20 yrs.	750	62.50	2.08
40 yrs.	375	31.25	1.04
50 yrs.	300	25.00	.83

COULD YOU AFFORD $1.00 A DAY TO BE ENERGY INDEPENDENT!

The limitations of solar are that you must pay up front for the system, maintain it, and normally can't run 100 AMP A.C. main service. You can't run heavy usage appliances such as electric heat or water heaters. Solar panels generate DC power which can be converted to AC current if needed. Therefore, your lifestyle will change some. **Ah...but think of the freedom!**

A solar system works to convert the energy of the sun into electrical energy This is called photovoltaics. Basically photovoltaics work as follows: Imagine a piece of metal. As it sits in the sun the metal warms. This warming is caused by the excitation of electrons, bouncing back and forth creating friction, and therefore heat. The solar cell merely takes a percentage of these electrons and directs them to flow in a path. A flow of electrons is called electricity. The outershell electrons are excited by particles of light and find the attached electrical circuit the easiest path to travel from one side of the cell to the other.

The basic method of photovoltaic modules or solar panels is simple. They convert sunlight into electricity. Wire conducts this electricity to batteries where it is stored until needed. On the way to the batteries, the electrical current passes through a controller (regulator) which will shut off the flow when the batteries become full. This electricity comes in the form of direct current or DC power. Many appliances and household electrical currents are set up for AC or alternating current. If you utilize an inverter it will convert the DC power from the solar panels into AC power. Many DC appliances are available also.

Solar power is not recommended to run heating loads. Appliances such as electric ranges, baseboard heaters or water heaters require large amounts of power. The amount of power required is not economically feasible with solar power.

The main factor to consider in deciding whether to utilize solar energy is insolation. Insolation is the determination of the intensity of sunlight in your area. This is measured by equivalent full sun hours. One hour of maximum, or 100% sunshine, is one equivalent full sun hour. You must also consider the amount of shading that your home gets from trees or mountains. If you live in an area that gets maximum sunlight, and you are on a flat plain with no interference from sunlight, you are in an excellent position to utilize solar power effectively.

The Basic Idea is Simple

Photovoltaic modules (solar panels) convert sunlight into electricity. Wire conducts the electricity to batteries where it is stored until needed. On the way to the batteries, the electrical current passes through a controller (regulator) which will shut off the flow when the batteries become full.

For some appliances, electricity can be used directly from the batteries. This is "direct current" and it powers "DC" appliances such as car headlights, flashlights, portable radios, etc. To run most appliances found in the home, however, we need to use "alternating current" or "AC", the type which is found in wall sockets. This we can produce utilizing an inverter which transforms DC electricity from the batteries into AC. The inverter's AC output powers the circuit breaker box and all the outlets in your home.

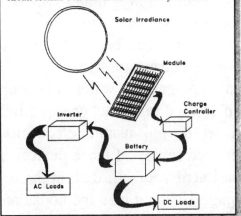

You can purchase a solar powered (non-electric) hot water system if you have sufficient capital to invest. The difference between a regular solar electric system and a solar hot water heating system is that the latter uses the sun as a heating source to heat water flowing in tubes with the solar panel. You could even install one of these systems yourself if you had adequate plumbing and technical skills. Though these systems may supply all of your hot water needs in the summer, you may have to rely on a back up heating system in areas where there are cold winters.

Wind power is something that some people have considered and utilized to generate electric power. Though this is feasible you need to be living in an area where there is considerable wind at all times of the year. If this is the case in your area you can investigate the possibilities of installing a windmill on your property. The wind mill can provide the mechanical power to run a motor that will provide electrical energy. As with other electrical generating systems, this electricity can then be stored in batteries for regulated use. Some windmills also pump water directly into a gravity flow tank which can be piped into the house.

There is also great interest in what are known as free energy devices. A free energy device is a device that produces more energy in output than it takes to run the device. The US patent office has said that this is impossible, and has refused to patent the creations of many inventors of free energy devices. Those that have been patented have never seen the light of day for consumer production and large scale manufacturing. In fact, Nikola Tesla invented an electric car at the same time as the creation of the internal combustion motor. But, as with the way of power monopolies, the large oil companies did not see a way to profit from his car, and his plans for the electric car were purchased and shelved.

There are many ways of converting electrical potential in the air into exciting electrons that can be conducted through wires to power electric appliances. Everything from rotating magnets to water implosion methods have been devised to extract energy from the ethers and convert it into usable electricity. If you are interested in any of these devices so that you can experiment yourself, look in the reference section on page 195 and read the books mentioned.

Self-Defense

Self Defense

You Have A Perfect Right to Defend and Protect Yourself

There is a lot of controversy today about what is the proper attitude toward self-defense. There are many in society that would have you believe that the government is there to protect you, therefore you need not have any form of weapon on your person or in your household. The idea is generated that weapons, particularly guns, are only created for one purpose, to injure or kill. That idea is taken further to imply that guns should be removed from society in an attempt to remove their potential for harm.

You read in the newspapers regularly about children who have accidentally harmed another by playing with guns. You read about how much violent crime is committed with firearms. This is intended to divert your attention from the fact that criminals create crime, not firearms. It is worth contemplating just how much of what the media tells you about guns and gun control is designed to persuade you to not get a firearm or to give up your firearm.

Listen carefully when you hear statistics of how many children or teenagers are killed each year by the mishandling of firearms. Statistics improperly presented can give a very distorted picture. Compared to automobile accidents the number of gun accidents is very small. The logic that is used here is that the gun is the killer. The gun is not the killer, the individual using the gun has the lethal intent. There are many instruments, including knives, axes and even automobiles that can injure or kill humans, yet it would seem absurd to remove them from society due to their potential for harm.

If you are confused or uncertain about gun control you may want to consider the following quote from James Madison written in the Federalist Papers, "Americans have the right and advantage of being armed - unlike the citizens of other countries whose governments are afraid to trust the people with arms." Many people are unaware that the real reason for the American Revolution was not solely taxation without representation. The British were also attempting to exert gun control in the colonies and deny the right to bear arms. This is why the right to bear arms is the Second Amendment to the Constitution. The Revolutionists knew that an unarmed populace is defenseless against an adversarial government.

Supreme Court Justice Douglas stated in 1963, "Should disarming the people while leaving the police armed be implemented, a powerful police state ultimately could strike blows at the right of the people to be secure from unreasonable searches and seizures. Indeed, extensive arms searches in private dwellings were made by the British in their aggression against Scotland, Ireland and America." Remember the saying,

"Power corrupts - absolute power corrupts absolutely."

We have included this chapter on self-defense in this book because we believe that being prepared for anything and everything is the wisest thing to do. Anything means that the government could change from an out of control state to one of total tyranny. If you were unprepared for a state of martial law all of your other efforts in preparing for self-sufficiency and sovereignty could be minimized. You would simply be told what to do and how to do it.

Consider it worth your effort to investigate all methods of   self-defense, and choose the method that feels right for you. There are many ways to defend yourself from aggression, from a firearm, crossbow, bow and arrow to the use of tear gas or pepper gas. You might also consider looking into the various forms of martial arts as a form of personal self-defense.

WHAT WEAPON TO CHOOSE

There are several options available for self-defense. Some of the more popular models are: handgun, rifle, shotgun, crossbow, bow and arrow, blow gun, tear gas or pepper sprays. Whichever weapon you are comfortable with is what you should obtain. To own a gun, for example, and be uncomfortable with using it, is not going to give you added security. You must decide at what level you are able to defend yourself. A crossbow, bow and arrow, blow gun or tear gas may not be as useful for a lethal confrontation as a gun would be. Each one of these methods only provides you with one opportunity to stop an aggressor. If the aggressor has a handgun as a weapon, you are very vulnerable unless you also possess a gun as a counterattack.

SHOTGUNS

The most popular and highly recommended home defense weapon is the 12 gauge pump shotgun, and preferably with an 18" barrel. This is the shortest barrel allowed by law. The advantage of a shotgun is that you can shoot repeatedly from the hip and you can spray your target. Plus the shot or pellets do not have a long range and their spray will not travel through too many walls or buildings. This eliminates the potential injury to others near by. This is more critical in cities and high population areas.

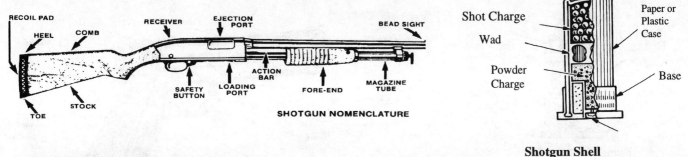

RECOIL PAD HEEL COMB RECEIVER EJECTION PORT BEAD SIGHT SAFETY BUTTON LOADING PORT ACTION BAR FORE-END MAGAZINE TUBE STOCK TOE

SHOTGUN NOMENCLATURE

Shot Charge — Wad — Powder Charge — Paper or Plastic Case — Base

Shotgun Shell

HANDGUNS

If you have decided that you are most comfortable with a gun as a weapon of self-defense, there are several things to consider before purchasing a gun. It is assumed that women should purchase a smaller more compact gun than perhaps a man would choose. This is faulty reasoning when considering the purpose for owning a gun. The purpose of a defensive handgun is to stop the act of violent aggression instantly. Both men and women have the same problem to solve at the moment of attack. Therefore, the proper weapon should be considered for the job.

The <u>standard rule</u> in choosing a gun is to find the <u>most powerful weapon that you can control</u>. If you are a women and you can control a .9 mm semi-automatic, then that is the gun you should purchase. Also consider whether you are purchasing a gun to carry on your person at all times, or simply to have in your home as a means to home self defense.

Handgun Options Chart

CALIBER	RECOMMENDED FOR:	COMMENTS
.44 MAGNUM	Hunting*	Not recommended for self defense
.357 Magnum	Specialized law enforcement*	Not recommended for self defense
.45 Auto	Home defense*	The gun to have if you are likely to be in a close-in gunfight. Recommended if you can handle it.
9 mm Auto	Home defense*	Generally too large for a carry gun. Useful for a gun to have in the home.
.38 Standard	Home defense*	Too large for a carry gun.
.38 Snubbie 2" barrel	Ideal for home and carry*	The most power in a compact size. The most popular carry gun.
.38 Auto	Home or Carry*	Low recoil. Minimum acceptable stopping power. Available only in an auto. Be aware of limitations.
.22 Auto	Home or Carry*	Low recoil makes it easy to learn to shoot. Be aware of limitations.
.25 Auto	Home or carry for those wanting the smallest, as well as one of the easiest guns to shoot.*	The least effective of all. Better than no gun.

*Beware - these bullets have the power to go through walls into adjacent rooms or homes.

159

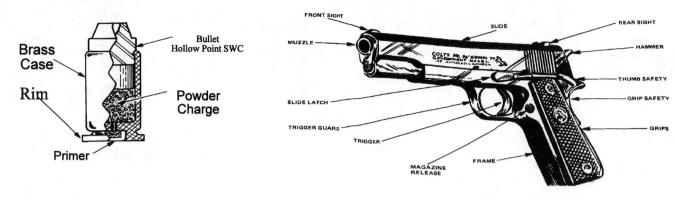

.45 Caliber Pistol

RIFLES

Modern assault rifles chambered for the .223 bullet are considered the first choice for any situation where human foes may be faced. Running a close second is the 30.06 bullet. Military rifles, though more expensive to repair, are also reliable and capable of taking extensive abuse before they fail. Military rifles can also be easily stripped and parts exchanged and reassembled. Assault rifles can require extensive work for repair problems. The main reason for a rifle is the extended range - very useful in hunting medium and larger game (pig, deer, etc.).

The first three choices of firearms for home defense are:

1. The 12 gage pump shotgun with 18" barrel.
2. .45 caliber hand gun - semi-automatic.
3. Rifle, .22 or .223 or larger.

Remember your choice of firearms depends upon how and where you intend to use it and your ability to control and handle it properly.

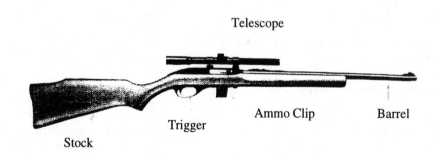

.22 Semi-Automatic

Lifestyle Recommendation Chart

The most popular gun for self defense for men and women is the .45 semi-automatic. Though this is a popular model, there are others to choose from. For a handgun you can consider a .22, .25, 357 magnum, .38 automatic or a .45. First consider the size of gun that you can comfortably control, and then within that range, which gun has the greatest stopping power. It would be wise to go to a local gun show or store and handle all the different varieties of guns. Once you have held a gun in your hand, you can determine whether you are comfortable with it as a weapon in a stressful situation. If a gun is too heavy for you to wield, it is useless as a weapon. Remember that when you will need to use a gun you will have to think quickly and be able to handle and use the gun with dexterity and accuracy. Handle each gun with this thought in mind. The next thing to consider when purchasing a gun is how powerful will it be in an emergency situation. Could it do the job in defending you and your family? Below is a chart of the different handguns on the market and what their potential stopping power is. A rating of 1 - 10 indicates 10 as the highest rating and 1 the lowest.

CALIBER	STOPPING POWER	CONTROL	COMMENTS
.44 MAGNUM	10	Very poor	Not recommended
.357 Magnum	10	Fair-poor	Not recommended
.45	9	Good	Recommended
9 mm	8	Very good	Recommended
.38 4" or 6" barrel	6	Very good	Recommended
.38 Snubbie 2" barrel	6	Fair-good	Recommended
.38 Snubbie	5	Excellent	Recommended
.22	3	Excellent	Recommended
.25	2	Excellent	Possible last choice

Training

An essential element in owning a gun is to be properly trained in its use. If you just own a gun and put it away in a drawer, assuming you will be safe in an emergency, you are fooling yourself. This is a false security, because a gun needs to be properly handled at all times. They are lethal weapons, and if improperly handled they are dangerous to the user as well as the target. If you are not willing to learn to use a firearm, you would be better off choosing another method of self defense.

Because the need for proper use of firearms is well known, the National Rifle Association has many programs and instructors who are available for learning to use and take care of your handgun or rifle. There are over 16,000 certified instructors. Simply write to: NRA Basic Firearms Education Department, NRA Headquarters, 1600 Rhode Island Avenue, NW, Washington, D.C. 20036. They will put you in touch with your local NRA branch, who can in turn guide you to a qualified firearm's instructor. Many areas have private gun ranges where you can receive instruction and practice. Once you have been properly instructed in using your firearm, you should then practice with some regularity.

Crossbows

Owning and using a crossbow is an option that many people prefer to owning a weapon such as a gun. A crossbow is quiet and appeals to those who don't like the kickback a handgun or rifle produces when shooting.

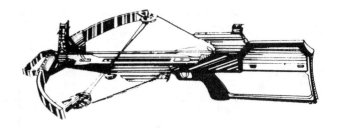

Modern Compound Crossbow

A crossbow is limited in its uses, particularly as a weapon of self-defense. But it is excellent for hunting game because it is quiet. Arrows or bolts, as they are called on crossbows, can hit their target without the explosive noise that guns or rifles make. Therefore, if you miss the first time, you haven't warned all the nearby game that you are in the area. You may reuse the bolts or arrows, but accuracy falls off with continued use. The bolts must be perfectly straight to hit the target.

It is estimated that approximately two to four months of practicing on a crossbow would make one proficient. They are easier to use and sight than a long bow. A bow can require a draw weight from 100 to 175 pounds. The maximum shooting distance for a crossbow is between 150 to 225 feet. Accuracy diminishes with the larger draw weight and longer distances. From 125 to 175 feet is a good average to bring down game or hit any other target.

Martial Arts

There are many forms of martial arts that can be used for self defense. These range from Aikido, Kung Fu, Judo, Karate, and the Ninja methods of invisibility. To obtain more information on these methods of personal self defense you should check locally with those who are teaching classes or who have attended classes in your area.

An additional advantage of learning any of the martial arts techniques is that they teach you how to achieve a one pointed focus. This ability will be important in difficult times, when all about you are in a state chaos, and it is necessary to remain calm and cool. The martial arts are also excellent training in sizing up your opponent before making any kind of move. If you can develop the clarity of thought to understand the mindset of one who is threatening you, you can be creative in designing a way to deter the threat. It is even possible to create a win-win situation for you and your opponent. There will be many people in stressful and catastrophic times that will be desperate to survive. They may do things that they otherwise wouldn't dream of. If you can size up your antagonist in a moment and know that there is another way to settle a matter, short of life-threatening measures, you both may walk away.

Sovereignty

Sovereignty

One of the most important elements in considering and preparing for survival of either a natural or man-made disaster is that of financial sovereignty. What do we mean by sovereignty? To be sovereign means to be free or independent. If you are financially sovereign then you have no debt and you own everything you have. In other words, you own your land and home, you own your vehicle and you own all of your personal effects. This is the ideal situation to be in.

It is a wise individual who is financially sovereign for they will not be caught short if the government decides to change the economic structure suddenly, or if there is an economic collapse along the lines of the October 1929 stock market crash. When the value of money plunges, as it did then, those who have all of their assets mortgaged out will be in a sorry state indeed. If you have a large debt outstanding, and the money you have has been so devalued that it cannot pay off that debt, you are in a position to lose everything that you hold in debt to another person or institution.

If you have a large debt on your home or vehicle and the economy collapses, the banking institutions, or whoever holds your mortgage, is in an excellent position to repossess your home. It may seem extremely difficult for some people to imagine owning their home without carrying some kind of mortgage on it, but it can be done. People have been lead by most financial advisers for the last thirty years to deliberately

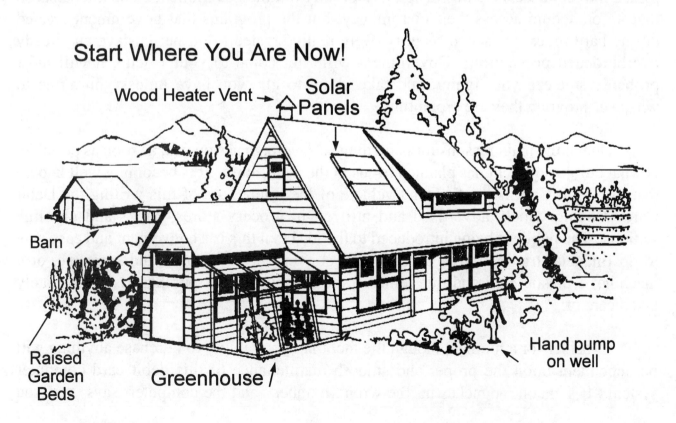

Start Where You Are Now!

Wood Heater Vent → Solar Panels

Barn

Raised Garden Beds

Greenhouse

Hand pump on well

carry as large a debt as possible on their home. They have been told that they can use their cash for other things. This line of thought has been generated and promoted by lending institutions and government agencies. These two structures profit greatly from your debt. Even the government gives a bonus on the sale of homes in the area of capital gains. If you buy a more expensive house with the earned profit from the sale of your home you are exempt from capital gains tax.

The mentality that accepts and extends itself into large debt has been supported heavily in the last quarter century. It is time that this kind of thinking be brought into balance. Remember that it is institutions, banks, insurance companies, and government agencies, that are so heavily in debt themselves that they will never see the light of day. These are the institutions that are encouraging the average citizen to live on borrowed money. Living on borrowed money is equivalent to living on borrowed time.

The example that the United States government has set for living in perpetual and increasing debt should be enough to frighten any sensible person into relieving himself of all debt. Particularly, since each of us pay dearly on the interest of the incredible and outrageous debt our government has and continues to create. It would be foolish to assume that this same government, out of control , will come to the rescue of the average citizen in times of economic collapse.

One need only look at recent history and see what happens when the economy is forced into collapse as it was in 1929. Not only did the government close the banks so that no one could access their own money, but the programs that government created during hard times, i.e. social security, were really created to further enslave an already overburdened population. Government will not come to your rescue, it will most probably squeeze you tighter, and take claim to all you have unless you agree to whatever program they are promoting.

One of the main reasons for becoming as sovereign as you can, as soon as possible, is what our government has planned for us in the near future. It is becoming well known that the Debit Card is the financial vehicle of the future. As of this writing the Debit Card is being widely advertised and utilized in grocery stores, banks and gasoline stations. The public is being introduced to the idea that this is a convenient and easy way to do financial transactions. It may seem convenient to simply hand someone, or a machine, a plastic card and out comes some money or your purchase is immediately taken care of.

Consider for a moment though the fact that your ability to purchase anything will be dependent upon the proper and smooth maintenance of this debit card computer system. If someone punches in the wrong number, and the computer says that you don't have sufficient money to purchase your food or gas, you will be denied these goods until the error is rectified. If someone steals your card they can purchase blindly from your card until your account is exhausted. If you lose your card you will be unable to purchase anything.

Under this system there will be no cash and carry. Within the Debit Card system your bank account records will be available and accessible to any government agency that wants access to this information and any creditor you have that wants to know what you are worth. Though this system may appear attractive and simple at first blush, realize that you are completely at the mercy of an electronic system and those who control that electronic system for everything you need to survive.

This kind of sovereignty means that you will be independent of the system. If you own your home there will be no institution or creditor that can come and repossess it if the economy collapses. The same is true for your car or any other personal items that are important to you. There will always be the consideration of property taxes, but the laws in each state are different on this. You might simply keep enough cash or gold coins on hand to prepay your property taxes, if this is allowable, in case the economy does fail. Most states allow three years of non-payment of property taxes before they consider a judicial foreclosure. It is highly possible that in the case of an economic collapse these rules will change. This is why many people keep a certain amount of gold on hand in gold coins so that they will still be able to pay property taxes with legal tender. You may also be able to pay off your mortgage with this gold. It is assumed that if the economy did collapse again, gold would not only be at a premium but it would soar in value. If this happens, even a nominal amount of gold purchased, at today's low prices could pay off all of your debts during the transition period to a new economy.

If the government is totally restructured, in the event of a man-made disaster or economic collapse, it is anyone's guess what the new rules will be. It is highly likely that martial law will be enacted for a period of time while everything is chaotic. In this event there is no way to predict how safe you will be personally or economically. It is absolutely certain though that even in the event of martial law, if the government has no legal ties to your property through debt, then the only way they could take it would be force. This is highly unlikely. In any event you will have to be prepared for anything. If you have paid for your property and your personal effects, then you are far ahead of the game in the event that society is seriously disrupted for any reason.

Ideally you would like to have land and/or a home in a rural area, far from any metropolitan area. There are still many beautiful and safe areas that are selling land for anywhere from $1,000 to $3,000 an acre. A purchase of the right five acres is easily sufficient for setting up a sovereign and safe lifestyle for future survival. If you already own a home, whether it is paid for or not, you might be able to trade up that home for something that is paid for in a country setting.

Whether your current home is paid for or not you may have equity in it beyond what your original down payment was. This, of course, will depend upon how long ago you purchased this home and what has happened to the real estate market in your area. Most people have a much greater potential for financial sovereignty than they realize.

If you took the equity in your current home and used it to purchase either a piece of land or a country home with it for cash, you would at least have one residence that was paid for. Even if you had to go into debt to do this, you could simply walk away from the home in debt in the event of a financial collapse and relocate to the home in a rural setting that was sovereign and paid for. This is one option.

Another option is that you can sell the home that you have now and buy property in the country with the profit you have realized. There are ways to avoid the capital gains tax on the sale of your current home. As of this writing the Internal Revenue Service allows two years for you to invest in another piece of property, to the extent that you have paid more for it than your original home. This is how you legally avoid capital gains tax. If you make a purchase that is more than what you sold you don't have to pay capital gains, because technically there are no capital gains. For example:

Your current home is currently worth $100,000
You owe only $40,000 on it
You sell it and realize a profit of roughly $50,000 after expenses
You purchase a piece of property in the country for $50,000
This property is free and clear of debt
You have two years to 'spend' $51,000 on this property so that this new property
  is worth more than the home sold for $100,000
The IRS has various publications that let you know what you can spend your
  money on that will legally increase the value of the new property, i.e.
  landscaping, structures added, structural changes, etc. The rule of thumb is that
  these changes must add to the value of the property or home and not be
  maintenance oriented.

In this way you can avoid capital gains and still own property free and clear. It will be potentially of lesser value than what you owned in the city. But in the long term your survival will not be measured in dollars. If you have sufficient capital in your home, and you can exchange this for land in the country, you may not even care about avoiding capital gains. Simply pay the gains tax and continue to improve your new residence, gearing for total survival. Always check with a competent tax expert for local and up-to-date IRS rules and regulations.

It is also possible for those who don't own property now, but do have some capital reserves, or can get access to some, to go in with others and purchase a piece of land with clear title. Even if this is just a beginning it would give you a place to retreat to in the event of a serious survival situation. It is more than nothing. With this focus in mind you can continue to add to the survival potential of the land with whatever resources you have, along with those you have invested with. Together you can build yourself a comprehensive retreat with long term survival and self-sufficiency in mind.

You are only as limited as you think you are. If you give serious contemplation to obtaining an alternative housing situation, if you are in the city, then you will begin to become aware of all of the potentials and possibilities awaiting you.   Don't underestimate the power of concentration on a potential idea. Be creative. You don't have to follow the route that everyone else has taken. There are many ways to create sovereignty for yourself, even some that haven't been invented yet. Be creative and courageous and you will invent something perfect for your situation. There are many stories of people who have accomplished and created extraordinary survival retreats. You can too.

How To Buy Country Land

When buying country land you need to become familiar with the area you are interested in relocating to. If you already have an area that you are excited about, or that you have spent considerable time in, you are ahead of the game. If you have visited a place only briefly, but know that you would like to settle there in the future, it would be wise to obtain a subscription to the local paper until you are able to make your move. This will acquaint you with property values and local county and city governments that you will be dealing with when purchasing your property. In this way you can keep a constant eye on what is available in the way of land values and property for sale.

There are a number of ways to purchase country land. If you decide to use a Realtor to help you find property, consider talking to several different Realtors. Realtors can have a tendency to concentrate on those properties which they or their company have as a listing. There may be properties for sale that you would never have heard about otherwise. You should also keep your eye on the local paper for properties that are for sale by owner. More and more people are deciding to sell by owner as the price of real estate commissions have risen. Remember, a Realtor works for the seller - not the buyer.

You may want to drive around a particular area that you are comfortable with and see if there are 'for sale' signs on any properties that you are interested in. There is also the possibility of land auctions. A land auction usually occurs because of non-payment of property taxes. These are handled through the county courthouse or by the lending institution that holds the mortgage. Land auctions are advertised in the local papers. You can obtain a property for a very good price this way, but you may also have to do a lot of legal paperwork to compensate for delinquent taxes and defaults on a mortgage.

Depending upon what your needs are in purchasing this land you should investigate a number of things before you actually put any money down on a piece of property. Check with the local Soil Conservation District. They can provide you with maps and information on the following specific areas:

     *Detailed soil identification
     *Seasonal high water table
     *Flood plains
     *Degree of slopes
     *Depth to bedrock
     *Potential for farming
     *Potential for forestry
     *Potential for septic systems
     *Potential for deep well water

All of these factors are important for the future use of any land for self-sufficiency purposes. Check also with the local city hall and ask to see a copy of the Uniform Building Code (UBC) for the area that you are planning to purchase. This will give you information on the permits that are necessary for any structures that you may want to build on the property, whether they are above ground or underground. Each city and county has its own version of the UBC that it incorporates into its local building codes. These codes are important for you to know. If you were to design a root cellar for example, or even a greenhouse that your city or county didn't consider up to code, you might have future problems if this were discovered.

You may not be interested in obtaining permits for everything that you are going to do on your property, but this is a matter of personal choice. Knowing what is expected of each property owner by local government is good knowledge to have.

Water

The water table in your area could be of critical interest to you for any future underground structure you have in mind. Never rely on the information of a Realtor or neighbor in determining what the ground water table is like. The local Water Rights District will have information, and possibly maps, to show what the ground water table is like in your area and what it has been like for the last fifty years. If you have a seasonally high water table this could be critical in deciding whether a piece of property will be useful in the long term.

If you are purchasing raw land you also need to be aware of the height of the water table for drilling a well. You should check with the Water Rights District and find out what the water levels are in your area. You can ask the closest neighbors how deep their wells are and get an approximation of how deep your well might need to be, but this is only partially accurate. Land can vary greatly, even between ten and twenty acres parcels.

If you are considering putting a hand pump on your well in the eventuality that electricity is not available, or if you never intend to have electricity, the depth of your well is critical. Ideally a hand pump will work on a well of from 30 to 100 feet. From 100 to 200 feet in depth requires much more hardware down the well, which in turn requires more work to pump water. Hand pumps can pump water beyond 200 feet, you just need to counterbalance the weight of hardware down the well and put in a smaller diameter cylinder. You can have a dowser come out to a piece of raw land and tell you what they think about the possibility of finding water and at what depth. This is risky though, unless the dowser has a good reputation.

Remember that water will be one of your most precious resources in times of personal survival. Having a good clean well with a hand pump on it could save your life. Don't assume that because you bought a piece of property with a year round pond or year round creek that this is yours to use as you choose. Many states have water rights laws that restrict you from using this water, even though it runs right through your land. You could be required to have special water rights permits. Montana, for example, actually owns the creek bed on every creek or stream in the state, regardless of who owns the surrounding surface land. To tamper with the creek bed, or alter it in any fashion, is a $500 a day fine. If you would like to use the creek for either drinking water, irrigation, fishing rights, or to water any animals, you must obtain special permits for these rights. And, if there are other property owners who are down stream from you who object to your using the water in any manner, they can object to the issuance of these permits. Water rights are held by date of issuance. Those who have had water rights the longest have the first say as to who and what use is considered down stream.

Make sure that the title to the land you have purchased has mentioned any water rights you are told verbally that you have. Though the seller may tell you you have access to a creek or stream in a certain manner, there should be a corresponding document paper from the Water Rights District that verifies this. If there isn't, check into it with the local authorities.

If you are purchasing a piece of property that already has an existing well there are a number of things to consider. Check if the source of water is shallow or deep. Does the water from this well need any kind of filtering? Is it being filtered at present? Is the water hard or soft? Is there an excess of iron in the soil? How many gallons per minute does the well pump? When was the last time the water was tested for contamination? It is usually standard practice to have a water test done by the county before escrow can close. If there is no well on the property research locally what costs are involved in drilling one.

Soil

If you are planning to feed yourself and your family on the property that you purchase you need to check out the conditions of the soil on this land. For farming an ideal soil would be moderately fine textured deep topsoil, teeming with bacteria, fungi and earthworms. It would be moist, well-aerated, well-drained and a have neutral ph. approximately 6.4ph. This soil is easy to cultivate.

To test the soil in your area do the following procedures:

Pick up a handful and see if it is friable (crumbles easily) and has a mixture of
   granule sizes.
Dig a hole and see how much loose soil there is before you hit tightly packed
   subsoil or clay.
Look for rotted leaves, stems and for earthworms.
The soil should make a ball easily but not be sticky and wet feeling.
If it is well aerated your shovel should penetrate easily. The soil is not stuck
   together.
Poorly drained soil has standing water. Pour on a bucket of water and see how
   well it drains.
Make a ball of earth and cut it in half. Place a piece of litmus paper between the
   two halves. Red means it is acid, blue means it is alkaline. Check this
   against a chart for values from 4.5 (very acidic) to 7.5 (alkaline).

Another simple test for soil acidity is to add a tablespoon of soil and a few drops of ammonia to a cup of rainwater. Stir. Check the water in two hours. Clear water indicates sweet, or alkaline soil; dark indicates a sour, or acidic soil.

Access To Land

Next consider what is your access to the land you are interested in. If it is a good county road then there is really nothing more to consider. If it is on a private road then you should ask to find out if there is a road maintenance agreement that has been written to maintain the road. A road maintenance agreement will not only cover the surfacing and grading of a road, but the plowing of a road in winter if you are in a cold climate. This could be a crucial point to consider before purchasing a piece of property. If there is no road maintenance agreement, and it is a private road, then you have no guarantee that you will have access to your property in winter unless you personally hire and pay for a snow plow yourself. If you really love a piece of property that is on a private road, and you have found out that there is no written road maintenance agreement, then ask to speak personally to several neighbors in the area. Find out if road maintenance has been a problem in the past, or if anyone on this road has the equipment to keep the road graded and plowed in the winter.

It is important to note when accessing your land whether you need to use an easement to get to your property. If you do, you need to have the conditions of the easement printed in the title report. Ask the Realtor for a preliminary title report before you consider purchasing, or make the purchase contingent upon there being a legal easement to your property. If a Realtor or seller tells you that they have been using this access route for a long time, but there has never been an easement, and that everything will be all right, don't believe them. Even a right of prescriptive easement (using an access road for more than seven years) can be challenged if the access road changes hands. Be clear with the seller that this is in writing and in the title report.

When purchasing a property investigate if there are any covenants that go with the property. Covenants are restrictions that have been placed on property by the county during subdivision or a local homeowner's association. These should be spelled out in the title report. Restrictive covenants may determine what kind of dwelling you can have on the land, what kind of animals you can have, how many, and other restrictions that could effect your future use of the land. Be clear with the seller that all covenants are reported to you and any proposed changes in covenants are given to you.

Land Use

When a purchasing a piece of property find out who your neighbors are and what they are doing with the adjacent land. One thing that some people never consider is that beautiful piece of woodland next to their future home, which is so beautiful and creates such a nice backdrop to their land. Is it owned by a private party or is it owned by a timber company? If it is not privately owned, is it owned by the state or federal lands management agency? The reason this is important is that you may be looking at a near future timber sale on the property next door. This could drastically alter not only your view, but the conditions of your land, and its value. If you have a creek on your property you have to make sure that those who cut the timber do it properly and don't destroy the stream.   Never assume that a logging company is going to follow all for the environmentally safe guidelines set up locally or by the federal government. If there is a proposed timber sale in the near future, and this would effect your use of your property, ask to talk to those who would be involved in the sale and see if it is imminent or can be diverted.

Zoning regulations can also be a consideration when purchasing a piece of rural property. Find out what the zoning is for the land you are interested in. Check with the local city hall and find out what zoning proposals are being considered and for what reasons. There may be special regulations that are involved in the zoning restrictions that you need to be aware of for future use.

Before putting any money down on property <u>please do your homework</u>. Use this checklist to assist you in determining whether this is the piece of property you want for you future potential use:

_____ **The deed is clear, there are no encumbrances.**
_____ **There is sufficient water available year round.**
_____ **The land has been surveyed and the stakes are posted.**
_____ **You are aware of any zoning or environmental restrictions which apply.**
_____ **There is legal access to the property.**
_____ **There is a road maintenance agreement.**
_____ **Power and telephone are available if you desire them.**
_____ **You are aware of any mineral or oil rights and who owns them.**
_____ **Are there any covenants that run with the land?**
_____ **The proper water rights have been deeded for a creek or pond.**

Reference
Section

Backpack List

Short Term Emergency

Water	Food	Shelter	Medicine	Clothing	Miscellaneous
Canteen - 1 qt.	MRE's	*Tent	First Aid Kit	Hat, Gloves	Compass
Water Filter	Freeze Dried	Emergency Blanket	Herbs	Waterproof Boots	Rope
*Water Purification Tablets	High Energy Snack Food	Poncho Rain Gear	Special Medications You may require	Extra Socks	Waterproof Matches
*Chlorine Tablets or H_2O_2	Vitamins and Minerals	Ground Cloth or Plastic	Sunscreen		Cooking Kit & eating utensils
	Herbs	*Sleeping Bag			Knives
	Charcoal Tablets	Zip Lock Bags			Paper, Pencil, Maps
		*Cold Weather Suit			Small Pen Light
					Shovel
					Walking Stick

*Optional

Water supplies should include a personal Katadyn pocket or mini filter plus a charcoal filter.

Food should be enough to last for at least 72 hours and require little or no cooking
Include a Hi Energy snack food like a pemmican bar, dried fruits, etc.

Shelter supplies should include zip lock bags to keep clothes and other items dry.

Clothes with a camouflage design are helpful.

Miscellaneous items should include toilet paper, soap (waterless preferred), matches, magnesium fire starter, fishing equipment, eating utensils, flashlight, Swiss army knife, can opener and a shovel. Back pack - camouflage or military color preferred.

Long Term Emergency or Group Back Packing Supplies

Water	Food	Shelter	Medicine	Clothing	Miscellaneous
Larger Katadyn expedition type	Dried Foods	Camo or Regular Tent	Large First Aid Kit	Extra shoes, boots	Small axe
	Food bag to hang in tree	Ground Pad	Homeopathic Kit	Extra Jackets	How-To books
	Cooking equipment	Blankets	Minor Surgery Kit		Solar Panels for recharging batteries
		Insect netting	Dental Kit		Weapons

Water supplies should include a charcoal filter and a larger expedition type Katadyn filter.

Food supplies should be hung in a tree to prevent wild animals from removing. Include cooking utensils and appliances that would cook for a group of people.

Shelter can be a military tent or larger family size one. Insect repellent and netting.

Medicine kit could include minor surgery provisions and a dental kit.

Clothes would include extra boots, gloves, hats and camouflage gear.

Miscellaneous gear including a small hatchet or axe, small saw, sling shot, air rifle, small caliber rifle or hand gun, extra ammunition or bow and arrow. You might want to pack some how-to books on survival for those who have not had a lot of camping experience. You could also include neatsfoot oil or waterproofing for your equipment. If you are staying for some time you will need soap, a sunscreen, cooking oil, dish detergent and aloe for burns. If you are going to be camped for an extensive period, take some solar panels to recharge batteries for flashlights, etc.

Special Considerations -
Children - consider any requirements for their age - diapers, formula, medical needs. Children's sizes of waterproof boots, rain coat, clothing or back pack.
Pets - Will they go along? Have you stored food for them? Can they carry their own food.
Special Medications - Each person responsible for their own, plan ahead.

General Preparedness Hints

- Be sure to store a good variety of high quality foods: freeze dried, air dried, grains, beans, seeds, MREs (Meals Ready To Eat): Use and experiment with the foods that you store. In this way you will understand how to prepare them and your family will be used to eating them. It takes approximately 3 months for your body to adjust to new ways of eating and about as long to adjust psychologically.

- Make certain you have a hand grain grinder in your storage plan, as wheat, corn, rye etc. need to be ground into flour. (There are several models available, see page 56-58.)

- Cooking oil is an important item to have in your storage program. Oil adds calories and flavor and also makes a great barter item. Buy extra oil that is sold from the store and place in your refrigerator unopened.

- A good variety of herbs, spices and flavorings are an absolute must in a viable storage program.

- When serving a bean dish include rice, wheat, or corn as part of the menu. Combining both grains and beans provides a nutritious meal complete in proteins.

- Add a little honey to your dehydrated vegetables to improve their flavor.

- To improve the flavor or powdered milk, add a small amount of vanilla and chill.

- Store your food in a cool, dry place away from sunlight to extend it's shelf life.

- Rotate your storage.

- To restore the mineral balance add blackstrap molasses to grains when cooking, especially if you are not sure that they are organically grown.

- The best way to buy grains or beans is nitrogen packed in poly buckets.

EARTHQUAKE / EMERGENCY CHECK LIST

KNOW HOW TO :

1. SHUT OFF GAS AT METER AND AT THE STREET IF POSSIBLE

2. SHUT OFF FUEL OIL AT TANK — if you use fuel oil

3. SHUT OFF PROPANE AT TANK — if you use propane

4. SHUT OFF ELECTRIC AT MAIN BOX IN YOUR HOUSE

5. SHUT OFF WATER AT MAIN VALVE IN YOUR HOUSE — or at the well if you have a well

DO PREPARE AND STOCK THE FOLLOWING

1. WATER STORED IN NON-BREAKABLE CONTAINERS @ 1 GAL. P.P.P.D. (per person PER day) minimum. Store at least 3 days worth - 1 month better.

2. FOOD - EASY TO FIX - NO COOKING REQUIRED: LIKE DRY CEREALS - CANNED GOODS, FREEZE DRIED - MRE'S (meals, ready to eat) - DEHYDRATED FOOD.

3. FIRST AID KIT - Get one with more than Bandaids in it. You will have to be your own medic.

4. SANITATION SUPPLIES - SOAP - WATERLESS SOAP (water is normally in short supply) MOIST TOWLETTES ETC. TO CONSERVE WATER. PAPER TOWELS, TOILET PAPER, SHOVEL, PLASTIC HEAVY DUTY GARBAGE BAGS FOR WASTE DISPOSAL ETC.

5. SHELTER - TARPS, PLASTIC, TENTS, HAMMER, NAILS, HEAVY DUTY TAPE.

6. FLASHLIGHT & SPARE BATTERIES OR RECHARGEABLE BATTERIES AND SOLAR PANEL.

7. RADIO - BATTERY OPERATED & SPARE BATTERIES - CANDLES & MATCHES.

8. SPECIAL MEDICATIONS YOU MAY NEED — STOCK UP AHEAD IF POSSIBLE.

9. WARM CLOTHES - EXTRA WARM BOOTS, COAT, GLOVES, HAT, LONG UNDERWEAR, RAIN GEAR.

10. SOAP, TOILET PAPER, PAPER TOWELS, GARBAGE BAGS, PLASTIC BAGS.

11. PERSONAL HYGIENE ITEMS — TOOTH BRUSH, COMB, WASH CLOTH, SOAP, ETC.

12. CAMPING TYPE STOVE AND FUEL - COOKING UTENSILS, SLEEPING BAGS, BLANKETS, SLEEPING PADS, TARPS, PLASTIC (minimum 3 mil thick) to cover stuff. Round up all your camping supplies and make a list.

EARTHQUAKE / EMERGENCY LIST CONTINUED

13. KEEP VEHICLE GAS TANK FULL - CAN BE USED AS EMERGENCY SHELTER - PARK IT OUT OF GARAGE /AWAY FROM TREES - BEWARE OF EXHAUST FUMES - Keep food & water here also. An additional emergency pack should always be kept in your car to be close at hand.

14. TOOL KIT - HAMMER, SAW, NAILS, CROW BAR, DUCT TAPE, ADJUSTABLE WRENCHES (Medium & large) PLYWOOD TO MAKE EMERGENCY SHELTER, TO REPAIR OR BOARD UP WINDOWS ETC.

15. EXTRA PET FOOD AND LEASH.

16. WATER PURIFICATION TABLETS AND / OR PORTABLE WATER FILTER.

17. REMOVE ALL GLASS FROM HIGH PLACES (Like in upper cupboards, shelves etc.).

18. PLAN ON NO ELECTRICITY OR PHONE FOR DAYS.

19. PLAN A FAMILY MEETING PLACE FOR AFTER AN EMERGENCY. HAVE OUT OF TOWN CONTACT (RELATIVE OR FRIEND) ACT AS A PLACE TO CALL TO RELAY MESSAGES BETWEEN THOSE WHO FIND THEMSELVES IN AN EMERGENCY.

20. BE SURE AREA IS FREE OF GAS OR EXPLOSIVE FUMES BEFORE USING ANY OPEN FLAME.

21. HAVE EXTRA CASH AVAILABLE — YOU MAY BE ABLE TO BUY SOME ITEMS IN AN EMERGENCY OR USE TO LEAVE TOWN. PUT SOME CASH IN YOUR EMERGENCY PACK ALSO.

22. DUFFEL BAG OR EQUIVALENT (to pack above in items in).

23. PACK ALL THE ABOVE (as much as possible in duffel bag or other similar heavy duty bag) AND KEEP NEAR FRONT DOOR OR TAKE IN CAR WITH YOU. IT IS AN EXCELLENT IDEA TO HAVE A SMALLER EMERGENCY PACK IN THE CAR AT ALL TIMES AND THE LARGER ONE AT HOME NEAR A DOOR SO YOU CAN TAKE IT WITH YOU ON THE WAY OUT.

THIS BASIC LIST IS TO GIVE YOU IDEAS ON WHERE TO START. BOOKS ARE AVAILABLE FOR MORE IN DEPTH STUDY. GIVE US A CALL FOR A FREE CATALOG ON EARTHQUAKE / EMERGENCY SUPPLIES AND OUR BOOK LIST. 72 HOUR KITS ARE AVAILABLE ALONG WITH WATER PURIFIERS AND EMERGENCY FOOD.

THIS LIST COMPLEMENTS OF:

THE SURVIVAL CENTER

PO. BOX 234
MCKENNA, WA 98558

206-458-6778 or 1-800-321-2900

"PREPAREDNESS PREVENTS PANIC"

Basic 72-Hour Emergency Kit

Why have a 72-Hour Emergency Kit? This will give you at least 3 days of being self-sufficient and reasonably comfortable in most emergencies. Many relief agencies say it will take at least 3 days to set up relief efforts, possibly longer, as we witnessed from the hurricanes in Florida.

A basic emergency 72-Hour Kit is a must in today's rapidly changing world. It is highly recommended by the Red Cross and other disaster relief agencies. Many school systems are requesting children have a 72 Hour Kit at school, as they plan to keep the children at school in the event of an emergency.

A 72 Hour Kit should be kept at school or work, near your most used entrance at home and one in your car. It is an excellent idea the keep one close by at all times.

The kits listed below will help you build your own or use as a reference when buying a ready made one. MRE's (Meals Ready To Eat) or other food rations may be added to extend the useful life of the kit or to care for others.

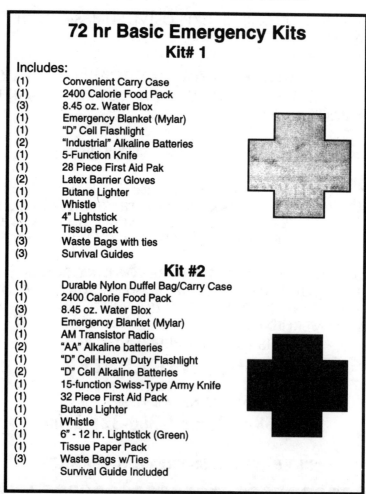

72 hr Basic Emergency Kits
Kit# 1
Includes:

(1)	Convenient Carry Case
(1)	2400 Calorie Food Pack
(3)	8.45 oz. Water Blox
(1)	Emergency Blanket (Mylar)
(1)	"D" Cell Flashlight
(2)	"Industrial" Alkaline Batteries
(1)	5-Function Knife
(1)	28 Piece First Aid Pak
(2)	Latex Barrier Gloves
(1)	Butane Lighter
(1)	Whistle
(1)	4" Lightstick
(1)	Tissue Pack
(3)	Waste Bags with ties
(3)	Survival Guides

Kit #2

(1)	Durable Nylon Duffel Bag/Carry Case
(1)	2400 Calorie Food Pack
(3)	8.45 oz. Water Blox
(1)	Emergency Blanket (Mylar)
(1)	AM Transistor Radio
(2)	"AA" Alkaline batteries
(1)	"D" Cell Heavy Duty Flashlight
(2)	"D" Cell Alkaline Batteries
(1)	15-function Swiss-Type Army Knife
(1)	32 Piece First Aid Pack
(1)	Butane Lighter
(1)	Whistle
(1)	6" - 12 hr. Lightstick (Green)
(1)	Tissue Paper Pack
(3)	Waste Bags w/Ties
	Survival Guide Included

Honey Substitution
(Conversion Chart for Recipes)*

Sugar	Honey	Subtract Liquid	or	Add Flour	Plus Soda
1 cup	**3/4 cup**	minus 1/4 cup	or	plus 4 T.	plus 1/4 t.
1/2 cup	**6 T.**	minus 2 T.	or	plus 2 T.	plus 1/8 t.
1/3 cup	**1/4 cup**	minus 1 1/2 T.	or	plus 1 1/2T.	plus 1/12 t.
1/4 cup	**3 T.**	minus 1 T.	or	plus 1 T.	plus 1/16 t.

Other sweeteners can be used also - fructose, date sugar, black strap molasses, maple syrup etc. Be creative if you want to avoid sugar. Date sugar and black strap molasses are best when baking.
*From Cookin' With Home Storage by Vicki Tate

Additional Uses for Vegetables:

Pizza: Top with chopped green pepper, broccoli, zucchini, or spinach.
Hamburger: Stuff patties with cooked shredded carrot, parsnip or spinach.
Macaroni and Cheese: Add some frozen vegetables to the cheese sauce.
Spaghetti: Stir some frozen vegetables into the tomato sauce.
Meat Loaf: Mix in chopped carrots, turnip, parsnips, rutabaga, or spinach.
Pita pockets: To top the filling with chopped cucumber, sprouts or cauliflower.
Pancakes: Stir mashed pumpkin or sweet potato into the batter.
Quick breads: Look for recipes that use corn, or shredded zucchini or carrot.
Soups: Add frozen or cut-up vegetables to your favorite cream soup.
Hot Dips: Serve a lemon dip with cool-enough-to-pick-up artichokes, asparagus or broccoli spears, string beans, cauliflower, or pea pods.
Cold dips: Serve a plate of raw vegetables, carrots, zucchini, broccoli, or kohlrabi.
Carrot chips: Thinly bias-sliced carrots with a vegetable peeler. Drop chips into ice water to crisp for dipping.

Reconstituting Dehydrated Foods*

Dried Food	Amount	Water	Yield
Apple Granules	1 cup	3 cups	3 cups
Apples Slices	1 cup	1 1/2 cups	1 1/2 cups
Apricot Slices	1 cup	2 cups	1 1/2 cups
Beets	1 cup	1 1/2 cups	2 cups
Bell Peppers	1 cup	1 1/2 cups	2 cups
Buttermilk	1 cup	1 1/2 cups	2 2/1 cups
Cabbage	1 cup	2 1/2 cups	2 cups
Carrots	1 cup	2 cups	2 cups
Celery	1 cup	1 cup	2 cups
Cheese	1 cup	1/3 cup	2/3 cup
Corn (Sweet)	1 cup	3 cups	2 cups
Dates	1 cup	1 cup	1 1/3 cups
Fruit Blend	1 cup	1 1/2 cups	1 1/2 cups
Gelatin	1 cup	4 cups	4 cups
Green Beans	1 cup	2 cups	2 cups
Margarine	1 cup	2 Tbs.	3/4 cup
Milk	1 cup	4 cups	4 cups
Onions	1 cup	1 cup	1 1/2 cups
Onions (Minced)	1 cup	1/2 cups	2 cups
Peach Slices	1 cup	2 cups	2 cups
Peanut Butter	5 Tbs.	4t. oil + 1/3 t. salt.	1/2 cup
Peas	1 cup	2 1/2 cups	2 1/2 cups
Potato Granules	1 cup	5 cups	5 cups
Sour Cream	1 cup	6 Tbs.	3/4 cup
Spinach Flakes	1 cup	1 1/2 cup	1 cup
Tomato Powder	1 cup	1 1/2 cup	1 13/4 cups

Emergency Substitutions*

Item	Amount	Substitute
Baking Powder	1 t.	1/4 t. soda and 1/2 t. cream of tarter
Butter or margarine	1 C.	1 1/2 C. margarine or butter powder
Chocolate (Unsweet.)	1 square	3 T. cocoa plus 1 T. butter
Cornstarch	1 1/2 t.	1 T. flour
Corn syrup	1 1/2 C.	1 C. sugar plus 1/2 C. liquid
Egg (Whole)	1 whole egg	2 egg yolks plus 1 T. water or 2 T. dehydrated eggs plus 2 1/2 T. water
Green pepper	1 medium	1/4 C. dehydrated green peppers
Milk, whole	1 C.	1/2 C. evaporated milk plus 1/2 C. water or 1 C. reconst. milk plus 2 T. butter
Onion	1 medium	1/4 C. dehydrated onion
Shortening or butter	1 C.	2/3 C. vegetable oil
Sour Cream	1 C.	1 C. milk plus 1 1/2 T. vinegar
Sugar	1 C.	3/4 C. honey (reduce liquid by 1/4 C. or add 1/4 C. flour)
		1 C. molasses
		1 1/2 C. carob syrup
		1 1/4 C. malt syrup
Sugar, powdered	1 C.	1 C. sugar and 1/2 t. cornstarch Blend in blender until powdered
White flour	1 C.	3/4 C. whole wheat flour
		7/8 C. rice flour
		1 C. corn flour
		1 C. corn meal unsifted
		1 1/2 C. rolled
		3/4 C. buckwheat
		1/2 barley flour
		3/4 C. rye flour
Yeast	1 package	1 T. yeast

Equivalent Measurements

Item	Equivalent
Bread	4 slices = 1 cup crumbs
Butter	1/4 pound = 1/2 cup
Cheese	1 pound = 4.5 cups grated
Flour, sifted	1 pound = 4 cups
Graham crackers	14 squares = 1 cup crumbs
Macaroni, uncooked	4 oz. = 2 1/4 cups cooked
Rice	1 pound = 2 1/3 cups
Spaghetti, uncooked	7 oz. = 4 cups
Sugar	1 pound = 2 cups
Sugar, brown	1 pound = 2 1/4 cups
Sugar, powdered	1 pound = 4 cups

Switching to Natural Foods - Recipe Substitutions

To Replace....	Use.....	Benefits.....
1 cup white flour in baking	1 cup minus 2 T. whole wheat flour; reduce oil by 1 T. per cup of flour; & increase liquid by 1/2 T. per cup of flour	Increased B vitamins, trace minerals, fiber and protein quality; more satisfying
2 T. flour from each cup when baking or kneading	2 T. wheat germ; or 2 T. soy flour; or 2 T. ground nuts or sunflower seeds	Increased protein quality, B vitamins, minerals, flavor
1 cup sugar in baking	3/4 cup raw honey; for each 3/4 cup honey either decrease liquid by 1/4 cup or add 1/4 cup flour	Avoid use of refined carbohydrates; add trace minerals; food stays fresh longer
1 cup sugar in baking	3/4 cup molasses & 1/4 cup sugar, decrease liquid by 1/4 cup for each cup of molasses, omit baking powder and substitute 1/2 tsp. soda for each cup molasses	Avoids use of refined carbohydrates; adds potassium, calcium, trace minerals, reduces calories by half
1 cup sugar in baking	1/2 cup maple syrup, reduce liquid by 2 T. for each 1/2 cup syrup	Avoids use of refined carbohydrates; adds potassium, calcium, trace minerals, reduces calories by half
1 cup sugar in baking	You can use barley malt, liquid or powder, rice syrup, date sugar or maple sugar granules as desired	Increased nutrients; decreased calories and refined carbohydrates
1 cup butter, margarine or solid vegetable shortening	7/8 cup cold processed vegetable or nut oils, preferably corn or sesame	Decreased saturated fats and cholesterol; decrease chemicals; increased unsaturated fat
1 T. solid fat in cooking	1 T. cold processed nut or vegetable oil; avoid high temperatures	Decreased saturated fats cholesterol, sodium & food additives, increased unsaturated fats
1 cup butter or margarine for spreading	1/2 cup butter softened whipped with 1/2 cup unsaturated cold processed oil. To increase benefits add 1 T. liquid lecithin & 100 I.U. natural vitamin E. (refrigerate)	Reduced cholesterol & saturated fats; increased unsaturated fats

Continued on next page

To Replace.....	Use......	Benefits......
1 T. flour as a thickener	1/2 T. arrowroot, kudzu, potato starch or 1/2 T. peanut butter	Reduced refined carbohydrates; fewer calories when using another starch; increased protein, B vitamins and minerals w/ peanut butter
1 cup milk	6 T. non-fat/non-instant dry milk powder and 1 cup water	Increased protein, calcium, riboflavin; saves money; long storage life
1 cup homogenized, pasteurized, Vitamin D. fortified milk	Raw cow, goat or sheep milk	Personal preference
1 cup milk	1 cup soy milk	Dairy free
1 tsp. sour milk, sour cream or buttermilk	1 tsp. yogurt	Increased B vitamins, easy to digest; saves calories & fat as sour cream substitute
1 cup sour cream when it will not be cooked	3/4 cup low-fat cottage cheese pureed with 1/4 cup yogurt or buttermilk	Reduced fat and calories, increased protein
1/2 cup whipped dream or whipped topping	1/2 cup non-fat dry milk powder whipped with 1/2 cup ice water and 1 T. orange juice	Less fat, calories and chemical additives, added protein, economical & convenient to store
Mayonnaise in salads and salad dressings	Equal amounts of yogurt and mayonnaise	Reduced fat, increased protein, calcium, B vitamins
Coffee lightener and non-dairy creamers	1 T. non-fat dry milk dissolved in 1 T. water	Avoid chemical additives & sodium, reduces fat, add protein & calcium; more economical
Cottage & ricotta cheese or mild cheeses in cooking	Equal amounts of tofu	Lower fat, calories, sodium; eliminates cholesterol; animal source free & lactose free

Continued on next page

Switching to Natural Foods - Recipe Substitutions (cont'd)

To Replace....	Uses.....	Benefit.....
1 whole egg in cooking	2 egg whites	Avoid cholesterol, reduces protein
1 egg in baking	1/2 tsp. baking powder & 2 T. soy flour	For egg-free diet
Up to 1/2 the ground meat in burgers, meat loaf and similar dishes	An equal amount of ground peanuts, cooked mashed soybeans, ground sunflower seeds, wheat germ, cooked grains such as brown rice, millet, bulgur wheat, rolled oats	Decreases animal fat, economical, increases fiber
All ground beef in burgers, meat loaf and similar dishes	Equal amount of cooked mashed soybeans, brown rice, millet, bulgur wheat, the addition of egg helps to hold it together	Free of animal fat and all negatives of animal protein, maintains high level of protein, vitamins and minerals, adds fiber
White rice	Equal amount of long, medium or short grain brown rice, increase cooking time by 20 minutes when cooked alone, 30 minutes when combined with other foods. Long grain is the most like white rice.	Increased protein, B vitamins, minerals & giver, richer taste, avoids refined carbohydrates and empty calories
1 lb. can cooked beans	3/4 cup dried or 2 cup cooked beans	Reduces sodium, avoids possible addition of additives & sugar, economical
1 tsp. salt	1 tsp. sea salt	Trace minerals present
1 tsp. salt or sea salt	1 tsp. powdered kelp; sesame salt; herbal seasonings (commercial or homemade)	Less sodium; more trace minerals, in some cases salt-free
1 square baking chocolate	3 T. carob powder plus 2 T. water	Avoid caffeine & reduces fat & calories

Centigrade - Fahrenheit Conversion Chart

Degrees Centigrade	Degrees Fahrenheit	Degrees Centigrade	Degrees Fahrenheit
0	32.0	26	78.8
1	33.8	27	80.6
2	35.6	28	82.4
3	37.4	29	84.2
4	39.2	30	86.0
5	41.0	31	87.8
6	42.8	32	89.6
7	44.6	33	91.4
8	46.4	34	93.2
9	48.2	35	95.0
10	50.0	36	96.8
11	52.0	37	98.6
12	53.6	38	100.4
13	55.4	39	102.2
14	57.2	40	104.0
15	59.0	41	105.8
16	60.8	42	107.6
17	62.6	43	110.0
18	64.4	44	111.2
19	66.2	45	113.0
20	68.0	46	114.8
21	69.8	47	116.6
22	71.6	48	118.4
23	73.4	49	120.2
24	75.2	50	122.0
25	77.0	100	212.0

WEIGHTS AND MEASURES
Metric System

LENGTH

UNIT	METRIC EQUIVALENT	U.S. EQUIVALENT
Millimeter (mm)	0.001 meter	0.03937 inch
Centimeter (cm)	0.01 meter	0.3937 inch
Decimeter (dm)	0.1 meter	3.937 inches
Meter (m)	1.0 meter	39.37 inches
Dekameter (dkm)	10.0 meters	10.93 yards
Hectometer (hm)	100.0 meters	328.08 feet
Kilometer (km)	1000.0 meters	0.6214 mile

WEIGHT OR MASS

UNIT	METRIC EQUIVALENT	U.S. EQUIVALENT
Milligram (mg)	0.001 gram	0.0154 grain
Centigram (cg)	0.01 gram	0.1543 grain
Decigram (dg)	0.1 gram	1.543 grains
Gram (g)	1.0 gram	15.43 grains
Decagram (dkg)	10.0 grams	0.3527 ounce avoirdupois
Hectogram (hg)	100.0 grams	3.527 ounces avoirdupois
Kilogram (kg)	1000.0 grams	2.2 pounds avoirdupois

CAPACITY

UNIT	METRIC EQUIVALENT	U.S. EQUIVALENT
Milliliter (ml)	0.001 liter	0.034 fluid ounce
Centiliter (cl)	0.01 liter	0.338 fluid ounce
Deciliter (dl)	0.1 liter	3.38 fluid ounces
Liter (l)	1.0 liter	1.05 liquid quarts
Dekaliter (dkl)	10.0 liters	0.284 bushel
Hectoliter (hl)	100.0 liters	2.837 bushels
Kiloliter (kl)	1000.0 liters	264.18 gallons

WEIGHTS AND MEASURES
U.S. System

LIQUID MEASURE	
4 Gills	1 Pint (pt)
2 Pints	1 Quart (qt)
4 Quarts	1 Gallon (gal)
31.5 Gallons	1 Barrel (bbl)
2 Barrels	1 Hogshead
60 Minims	1 Fluid dram (fl. dr.)
8 Fluid drams	1 Fluid ounce (fl. oz.)
16 Fluid Ounces	1 Pint

LINEAR MEASURE	
1 Mil	0.001 Inch (in)
12 Inches	1 Foot (ft)
3 Feet	1 Yard (yd)
6 Feet	1 Fathom
5.5 Yards	1 Rod (rd)
40 Rods	1 Furlong
5280 Feet	1 Mile (mi)
1760 Yards	1 mile

SQUARE MEASURE	
144 Sq. inches	1 Sq. foot
9 Sq. Feet	1 Sq. Yard
30.25 Sq. Yards	1 Sq. Rod
160 Sq. Rods	1 Acre
640 Acres	1 Sq. Mile

APOTHECARIES' WEIGHT	
20 grains	1 Scruple
3 Scruples	1 Dram (dr)
8 Drams	1 Ounce (oz)
12 Ounces	1 Pound (lb)

AVOIRDUPOIS WEIGHT	
27.34 grains	1 dram
16 Drams	1 Ounce
16 Ounces	1 Pound
2000 Pounds	1 Short Ton
2240 Pounds	1 Long Ton

CUBIC MEASURE	
144 Cubic inches	1 Board foot
1728 Cubic Inches	1 Cubic Foot
27 Cubic Feet	1 Cubic Yard
128 Cubic Feet	1 Cord

DRY MEASURE	
2 Pints	1 Quart (qt)
8 Quarts	1 Peck (pk)
4 Pecks	1 Bushel (bu)
3.28 Bushels	1 Barrel (bbl)

WEIGHTS AND MEASURES

COOKING MEASURES	
Dash	Less than 1/8 Teaspoon (Pinch)
3 Teaspoons	1 Tablespoon (1/2 fluid ounce)
2 Tablespoons	1/8 Cup (1 fluid ounce)
4 Tablespoons	1/4 Cup (2 fluid ounces)
5 1/3 Tablespoons	1/3 Cup (2 2/3 fluid ounces)
8 Tablespoons	1/2 Cup (4 fluid ounces)
10 2/3 Tablespoons	2/3 Cup (5 1/3 fluid ounces)
12 Tablespoons	3/4 Cup (6 fluid ounces)
14 Tablespoons	7/8 Cup (7 fluid ounces)
16 Tablespoons	1 Cup
1 Gill	1/2 Cup
1 Cup	8 fluid ounces
2 Cups	1 Pint

Preparedness Checklist

FOOD STORAGE	FOOD PREPARATION
Freeze Dried	Grain Mills
Air Dried	Juicers
MRE's	Grinders
Nitrogen packed grains, beans, seeds	**WEAPONS (We don't carry these)**
Canned Foods (wet pack)	Hand Gun
WATER	Rifle or Shotgun
Storage Containers	**FOOD PRESERVATION**
Filter	Waterbath Canners
Purification Tablets	Pressure Canners
MEDICAL SUPPLIES	Dehydrators
First Aid	Barrels
Retreat Kits	**SOLAR SUPPLIES**
Homeopathic First Aid Kit	Solar Panels
SHELTER	Inverters
Retreats	Appliances
Underground Shelter	Power Modules
Safe Place	Battery Chargers
MISCELLANEOUS	**LIGHTING SUPPLIES**
Soap	Brass Lamps
Toilet Paper	Kerosene Burner
Saws	Oil Lantern
Axes	Candles
Garden Tools	**WILDERNESS SUPPLIES**
Generators	Knives
COOKING SUPPLIES	Machetes
Wood Stoves	Sleeping Bags
Coleman Stoves	Tents
Alcohol Stoves	Backpacking Supplies
SURVIVAL CENTER CATALOG $2.00	

The Survival Center
P.O. Box 234
McKenna, WA 98558

Call
1-800-321-2900
Or
1-206-458-6778

For All of Your Survival Needs

Reference Section

Food Storage
Stocking Up, by Carol Hupping; *Food Storage Handbook,* by Cathy and Dan Brimhall; *Cooking with Home Storage,* by Vicki Tate and Peggy Layton; *Crude Black Molasses,* by Dr. John Lust; *Cooking with Honey,* by Joanne Barrett; *Home Food Dehydrating,* by Jay and Shirley Bills; *Bee Prepared with Honey* by Arthur W. Andersen; and *Keeping the Harvest* by Nancy Chioffi & Gretchen Mead.

Water Storage
Home Water Supply: How to Find Filter, Store and Conserve It, Garden Way Publishing; *Manual of Individual Water Supply Systems,* Washington D.C. EPA; *Water Supply for Rural Areas and Small Communities,* by Edmund G. Wagner and *How Safe Is Your Water?* by Kenneth M. Stone.

Medical Supplies & Sanitation
Emergency Medical Treatment: Adults, by Stephen Vogel; *Emergency Medical Treatment: Children,* by Stephen Vogel; *The SAS Survival Handbook,* by John Wiseman; *Where There is No Doctor,* by David Werner; *Where There is No Dentist,* by Murray Dickson; *Homeopathic First Aid Manual,* by M. Moore; *Homeopathic Medicine For Women,* by Dr. Trevor Smith; *Homeopathy and Medicine of the New Man,* by George Vitkoulkas; *The Herb Book,* by John Lust and *The Handbook of Alternatives to Chemical Medicine,* by Mildred Jackson and Terri Teague.

Shelter
Building Small Barns, Sheds & Shelters by Monte Burch; **Nuclear War Survival Skills** by Cresson H. Kearny.

Grains
The Bread Book by Thom Leonard; *Uprisings The Whole Grain Baker's Book* by the Cooperative Whole Grain Educational Association; and *Bread Book* by The Laurel Kitchen.

Processing Foods
Fresh From a Vegetable Garden by Meredith McCarty; *Putting it up with Honey* by Susan Geiskopf; *The Canning, Freezing, Curing & Smoking of Meat, Fish & Game* by Wilber F. Eastman, Jr.; *Fun with Fruit Preservation* by Dora D. Flack; and *Stocking Up* by Carol Hupping.

Household Products
691 of the Best Household Tips by Richard L. Scott; *Too Busy to Clean?* by Patti Barrett; *The Art of Soap Making* by Merilyn Mohr; *The Guide to Self-Sufficiency* by John Seymour; *Back to Basic* by Reader's Digest.

Tools
Simple Home Repairs by Storey Communications, Inc.;   and *Axes and Chainsaws* by Storey Publications.

Homesteading
Woodstove Cookery by Jane Cooper; *Back to Basics* by Reader's Digest; *Hard Times Handbook* by Keith & Irene Smith; *The Guide to Self-Sufficiency* by John Seymour.

Alternative Energy
Handbook of Homemade Power by The Mother Earth News; *Solar Projects for Under $500,* by Mary Twitchell; and *What To Do When the Power Fails,* by Mary Twitchell.

Self-Defense
The Crossbow as a Modern Weapon, by Galen L. Geer; *Firearms for Survival,* by Duncan Long; and *Self-Defense Needs No Apology,* by Jan Jones.

Glossary

Air-Dried - Food that has been dried by slicing, dicing or cutting into strips. These pieces are then dried in the air.

Alternator - An electric generator for producing alternating electrical current.

Botulism - This is a deadly form of bacteria. It begins as spores in food that is spoiled. It is odorless and tasteless.

Cistern - This is a method of capturing water that is flowing at ground level or through a pumped system. It acts as a holding tank for water.

Freeze Drying - This is a form of vacuum sublimation. Foods are flash frozen at -50°F, then placed in a vacuum chamber where radiant heat is applied. This turns the frozen water content directly into a vapor, which is vacuumed away.

Fruit Leather - This is fruit that has been ground up into a dry liquid, spread out as thinly as possible and either air dried or put in an electric dehydrator. The fruit will turn into a sheet or leathery fruit.

Generator - A machine in which mechanical energy is changed to electrical energy.

H_2O_2 - Hydrogen peroxide. Use 35% food grade. Used to keep water purified for long term storage.

Insolation - The determination of the intensity of sunlight in your area.

Jerky - This is dried and seasoned meat that has been air dried or dried in an electric dehydrator. The meat is sliced very thin, marinated in spices for several days and then dehydrated.

MRE - Meal Ready To Eat. Military Food Rations.

Nitrogen Packed - Nitrogen is an inert gas that won't react with foods. Food to be stored is first vacuum packed and then nitrogen is backflushed in the container to prevent oxygen retention.

Photovoltaic - Energy produced by the sun that is converted into electricity and used in solar applications.

Pigtail Adapter - An adapter that interlocks with another electrical plug. Easy to hook up to generator or extension cord for emergency operations.

Sand Point - This is a type of shallow well. A special fitting such as a conical sieve is attached to the end of the well pipe that reaches into the ground. The sieve acts as a filter. This is possible for water that is only to a depth of thirty or less feet.

S.C.U.P.P. - Self-Contained Underground Power Plant.

Self-Sufficient - Capable of providing for one's own needs. Ability to maintain oneself without outside aid.

Smoke House - A smoke house is a chamber that is used to allow smoke to travel through. The smoke dehydrates the food and adds a bit of flavor, depending upon the wood that is used to create the smoke.

Springhouse - This is a structure that is constructed on or near a source of running water, such as a stream or creek. The water flows through the springhouse and helps to keep food cool.

Stearin - This is a powder that is added to paraffin in making candles. It helps to harden the wax.

Trench Shelter - This is a special kind of underground shelter that uses a shallow trench covered with logs and plastic for protection in the event of an emergency.

Water Bath - This is a method of home canning that uses a water bath canner.

Waterglass - This is a method of preserving eggs. A crock is filled with sodium silicate and eggs that are at least 12 hours old are immersed in this liquid of 1 parts sodium silicate to 11 parts water. The eggs will keep for at least one year in this solution.

Index